After the Holocaust
The Book of Job, Primo Levi, and the Path to Affliction

The Holocaust marks a decisive moment in modern suffering in which it becomes almost impossible to find meaning or redemption in the experience. In this study, C. Fred Alford offers a new and thoughtful examination of the experience of suffering. Moving from the Book of Job, an account of meaningful suffering in a God-drenched world, to the work of Primo Levi, who attempted to find meaning in the Holocaust through absolute clarity of insight, he concludes that neither strategy works well in today's world. More effective are the day-to-day coping practices of some Holocaust survivors. Drawing on testimonies of survivors from the Fortunoff Video Archives for Holocaust Testimonies at Yale University Library, Alford also applies the work of Julia Kristeva and the psychoanalyst Donald Winnicott to his examination of suffering, a topic that has been and continues to be central to human experience.

C. Fred Alford is Professor of Government and Distinguished Scholar-Teacher at the University of Maryland, College Park. A recipient of three awards from the Fulbright Commission, he is the author of more than a dozen books in moral psychology – most recently, *Psychology and the Natural Law of Reparation*.

After the Holocaust

The Book of Job, Primo Levi, and the Path to Affliction

C. FRED ALFORD
University of Maryland

CAMBRIDGE
UNIVERSITY PRESS

CAMBRIDGE UNIVERSITY PRESS
Cambridge, New York, Melbourne, Madrid, Cape Town, Singapore, São Paulo, Delhi

Cambridge University Press
32 Avenue of the Americas, New York, NY 10013-2473, USA

www.cambridge.org
Information on this title: www.cambridge.org/9780521747066

First published 2009

Printed in the United States of America

A catalog record for this publication is available from the British Library.

Library of Congress Cataloging in Publication data

Alford, C. Fred.
After the Holocaust : the book of Job, Primo Levi, and the path to affliction /
C. Fred Alford.
    p.   cm.
Includes bibliographical references and index.
ISBN 978-0-521-76632-6 (hardback) – ISBN 978-0-521-74706-6 (pbk.)
1. Suffering – Religious aspects – Judaism.   2. Suffering – Biblical teaching.   3. Bible.
O.T. Job – Criticism, interpretation, etc.   4. Levi, Primo.   5. Holocaust, Jewish
(1939–1945).   6. Holocaust survivors – Interviews.   I. Title.
BM645.S9A44   2009
296.3′1174 – dc22   2008048864

ISBN   978-0-521-76632-6 hardback
ISBN   978-0-521-74706-6 paperback

To my mother, who understood affliction.

Contents

Preface

The list of those to whom I owe thanks for making this book possible is longer than usual.

My brother-in-law, Ira Wolfson, helped introduce me to the complexity of the Book of Job.

My colleague, Jeffrey Herf, of the History Department at the University of Maryland, College Park, first suggested that I compare Job with Primo Levi. It turned out to be an enormously fruitful suggestion, although I'm not quite sure what he will think of the result.

My departmental chair, Mark Lichbach, has supported and encouraged my work in ways big and small.

My colleague, Jim Glass, once again read the entire manuscript and once again helped me retrieve the key argument, which it is all too easy to lose in the details.

Matt Bowker, a former graduate student and now a professor in his own right, helped me teach an honor's seminar on affliction and taught me much of what I know about Camus.

Aryeh Botwinick, a colleague at Temple University, helped me with the biblical Hebrew, as well as encouraging me along the way. Sara Botwinick, his wife and a social worker for a Jewish social services agency, helped me understand the vulnerability of the aging survivor.

I owe a particular debt of gratitude not only to the Fortunoff Video Archives for Holocaust Testimonies at Yale University Library, but also to the lead archivist there, Joanne Rudof. We had several valuable discussions, and she taught me how important it is not to remain transfixed by the suffering of the witness but rather to look beyond to those who caused this suffering and why.

Several times, Ms. Rudof served as a conduit between the eminent Holocaust scholar Lawrence Langer and me. I would ask a question, Ms. Rodof would ask Professor Langer, and Ms. Rudof would transmit his answer. It took me a while to realize that this mediated form of communication was my own choice because Langer had made his email address available to me. Whether it was the "anxiety of influence" or my reluctance to disagree with a man who knew so much more than I about the survivor experience that held me back, I am not sure. In any case, I learned much this way, and whereas I believe that I emphasize the creativity of the survivors' response more than is apparent in Langer's work, I have no doubt that I owe Langer more than I know.

It is difficult to explain to one who has not had the experience how compelling watching videotaped interviews with Holocaust survivors can be. For most of the interviews in the Fortunoff Video Archives (some were conducted by other organizations), the camera focuses exclusively on the witness for the entire interview, usually focusing on the face, sometimes moving back to take in the entire body, occasionally moving between face and hands. The interview has no time limit but generally runs between one and two hours. Good interviewers (who far outnumber the bad) ask relatively few questions and tolerate long, anguished silences; the result is that while watching the interview on a television monitor, I was the one drawn in. More than once, I was momentarily disoriented when, at the end of the interview, the camera pulled back, revealing the subject together with the interviewers. I felt as if I had been there alone with the witness.

This is not an unusual experience when watching a good movie or play. At the theater, my wife loves to sit in the first row so she can feel herself part of the action, almost imagining she is on stage with the actors. She wants to lose herself in the play for a couple of hours. That's why people go to the movies or theater. It doesn't seem like anyone would want to do that while watching Holocaust testimony for six hours a day, five days a week, and then going back to a hotel room at night and spending another few hours typing up one's notes in order to keep it all straight. However, although I didn't want to do it, I sometimes felt I almost had to do it – more than that I cannot explain.

My research in the Fortunoff Video Archives for Holocaust Testimonies at Yale University Library, as well as my subsequent writing of the chapter devoted to this testimony, was supported by a General Research Board Award from the Graduate School of the University of Maryland, College Park.

My wife, Elly, understands the importance of this work, even as she finds it difficult to discuss.

On hearing me complain about how difficult it was to listen to Holocaust testimony all day and then write about it at night, my friend, Milton Teichman, said something along the lines of, "If they can endure it and live to tell about it, you can sit in a comfortable room and watch and write about it." He is absolutely right. It is unbecoming to complain about the hardships of viewing Holocaust testimony.

Another friend, Cheryl Dockser, pointed out the passage in Philip Roth's *Exit Ghost*, referring to Primo Levi's suicide.

My editor at Cambridge, Beatrice Rehl, worked with me longer on this book than I had a right to expect, especially when I ended up rewriting it in midstream. It is a pleasure to work with her.

A couple of anonymous reviewers for Cambridge were enormously helpful.

I regret that I was unable to use material from several conversations with Holocaust survivors in which I was fortunate to participate. One survivor was imprisoned at the same slave-labor camp as Primo Levi. Those conversations, however, prepared me for the Fortunoff Video Archives for Holocaust Testimonies, and nothing I saw or heard in those testimonies fails to fit the general tenor of the conversations in which I participated.

1

Introduction

The great mystery of human experience, Simone Weil wrote, is not suffering but rather affliction (Weil 1977a, 441). For most of us, there is not much difference, except perhaps in degree and duration. Affliction is suffering that is extended over time, suffering that seems to blight some lives even at birth, suffering that seems beyond human comprehension and endurance. For Weil, an unorthodox religious essayist, affliction is a special quality of suffering. In affliction, distress of the soul and social degradation are at least as important as physical suffering (Weil 1977a, 452). For Weil, affliction shares the quality of what Julia Kristeva (1982), psychoanalyst and literary critic, called abjection. Abjection means more than the loss of pride, dignity, and worth; in abjection, one loses more than one's sense of self-worth – one is in danger of losing one's self.

Even as they share little else, both Weil and Kristeva (1996, 213–15) understand the attractions of abandoning the self. The difference is that for Weil, affliction may have the quality of a blessing. For Weil, affliction is suffering made meaningful. Affliction makes suffering meaningful when it fosters the experience of *metaxy* (*metaxu*), a Platonic term adopted by Weil (1977d) to signify that one is not the center of the world, that the center is outside – indeed, all around. The proper human attitude, even in the midst of suffering, is one of awe, acceptance, and wonder:

Unless constrained by experience, it is impossible to believe that everything in the soul – all its thoughts and feelings, its every attitude towards ideas, people, and the universe, and above all, the most intimate attitude of the being towards itself – that all this is entirely at the mercy of circumstances. Even if one recognizes it theoretically, and it is rare indeed to do so, one does not believe it with all one's soul. (Weil 1977a, 457)

In her last years, Weil was attracted to the Upanishads, believing that the self was an illusion that must be banished to make true contact with Brahman. Elsewhere, Weil gave a more familiar Catholic explanation for self-denial, although perhaps the familiarity is deceiving, stemming from ordinary religious terms such as sin. "The self is only the shadow which sin and error cast by stopping the light of God. . . . The sin in me says I" (Weil 1963, 27).

We can interpret Weil, however, in a more secular vein. It is good to know and accept one's nakedness and vulnerability before fate and might so that we do not become what Weil called a Pharisee, one who worships the empire of might, social power in all its forms. This is perhaps the hardest thing for humans to do: not to confuse goodness and might – that is, not to worship might because it is might. Yet, it is essential if we are to become just and good. "Only he who knows the empire of might and knows how not to respect it is capable of love and justice" (1977b, 181).

The explicit rejection of social idolatry unites Weil, Primo Levi, and Job, setting Job against his three friends, for whom social prestige is a sign of God's blessing. However great, Job's suffering was meaningful. In the end, he experienced metaxy and learned a great lesson. The lesson of Auschwitz is that extreme suffering can be rendered meaningless[1] – not only for those who undergo the suffering but also for the generations that follow. This is captured in a camp guard's response to Primo Levi, who asked, "*Warum?*" when a guard snatched an icicle out of his hand just as he was about to suck on it to relieve his terrible thirst. "*Hier gibt es kein warum,*" answered the guard: "Here

---

[1] Here and throughout, unless otherwise noted, Auschwitz refers not only to the death camp but also more generally to the machinery of degradation and death that was the Holocaust. When speaking specifically about the death camp in German-occupied Southern Poland, I refer to Auschwitz-Birkenau. Chapter 3, based on the testimony of survivors, is a partial exception. When witnesses are quoted or paraphrased as referring to Auschwitz, they generally mean the concentration and extermination camp, Auschwitz-Birkenau. I leave their references unchanged.

there is no why, no reason, no point in asking because there is no answer" (Levi 1996, 29).

It is well to remember that there were men and women at Auschwitz who found meaning in their suffering, so that one might say that their suffering became affliction (Levi 1988, 146). For the majority of inmates, however, the suffering of Auschwitz was soul-destroying. Levi stated it this way in imagining what the Nazis might say to their victims: "'We, the master race, are your destroyers, but you are no better than we are; if we so wish and we do wish, we can destroy not only your bodies but also your souls, just as we have destroyed ours'" (Levi 1988, 53–4). Not for a moment does Levi doubt that this is true.

One might argue that Levi's books prove that it is not true, at least not for every survivor. However, Levi's suicide seemed to demonstrate that the reach of the Nazis was unlimited. If Levi could not save his own precious and gifted soul, then who could?[2] As Eli Wiesel said, "Primo Levi died at Auschwitz forty years later" (Gambetta 1999).

Not every survivor failed to escape the long reach of Auschwitz. Chapter 3 is based on my research in the Fortunoff Video Archives for Holocaust Testimonies at Yale University Library, which contain interviews with more than five thousand survivors. I have drawn on the memoirs of several survivors as well as the research of psychoanalytic and cognitive psychologists. Whereas every survivor is wounded, many creatively come to terms with their wounded selves, finding ways of living with parts of themselves that are essentially intolerable. As Charlotte Delbo (2001, 2–3) said in her memoir, "I don't live with Auschwitz. I live next to it." Delbo found a way to double – that is, to live with a part of her self that she cannot live with and cannot live without – at least not without destroying the person whom she had become. This seems to be the strategy of most survivors.

It was not the strategy of Levi, who fought so terribly hard in his written works to come to terms with his Auschwitz double. "'All sorrows can be borne if you put them into a story or tell a story about them.' The story reveals the meaning of what otherwise would remain an unbearable sequence of sheer happenings" – so said Hannah Arendt

---

[2] In accord with Levi's intent, I understand the term *soul* in terms of the original Greek term *psyche*, which may be rendered as self, psyche, or soul.

(1968, 104). It's not true. Certainly, it is not true for many survivors, and evidently it was not true for Levi, although much remains uncertain. There are reasons other than the weight of Auschwitz that he might have killed himself, a remote possibility that he didn't; and the rush to judgment has more to do with his audience's need for narrative closure than with the reality of any man's or woman's life. With the help of Cynthia Ozick (1989, 46–8), among others, Levi became a man of repressed rage on whom Auschwitz finally took its inescapable revenge forty years later. If only he hadn't been so humane.

The term *inescapable* in the previous paragraph is from Natalia Ginzburg, who states that "of those years [in Auschwitz-Birkenau] he must have had terrible memories: a wound he carried with great fortitude, but which must have been nonetheless atrocious. I think it was the memory of those years which led him towards his death" (Gambetta 1999). Drawing on the Fortunoff Archives testimonies, as well as several memoirs, I suggest that there is no single experience of the Holocaust even for a single individual. The experience of the Holocaust changes, sometimes radically, over time, particularly as the individual ages and new experience changes the self's experience of the old.

What about my narrative? Do I escape narrative's rush to judgment? The reader is in the best position to answer this question. In any case, one should be constantly aware of the way in which narrative itself wants closure more than is good for those who would try to understand. The storyteller should aim to resist this pressure, without detaching himself or herself from the narrative (i.e., without becoming ironic) or imagining that there is somewhere outside the narrative to stand. For I too have a story to tell, one in which Levi identifies with the unmerited sufferings of Job. Unlike Job, however, Levi is unable to prevent himself from being drawn into the Black Hole of depression and meaninglessness. (Toward the end of his life, Levi became fascinated with the astrophysical phenomenon of Black Holes.)

I turn to the Book of Job for several reasons. First, Job was afflicted; however, unlike the suffering of the survivors of the Holocaust, Job's affliction is widely held to be meaningful. Job, in other words, comes closer to those few believers, about whom Levi wrote, who saw their suffering within the framework of a vaster, more meaningful universe:

> The believers lived better. Both [Jean] Améry and I observed this.... Their universe was vaster than ours, more extended in space and time, above all more comprehensible: they had a key and a point of leverage, a millennial tomorrow so that there might be a sense to sacrificing themselves.... [even] their hunger was different from ours. It was a divine punishment or expiation, or votive offering.... Sorrow, in them or around them, was decipherable and therefore did not overflow into despair. (Levi 1988, 146)

Whereas there were certainly believers among witnesses whose testimony I viewed, none referred to the type of spiritual meaning Levi found among a few inmates. On the contrary, many spoke of days (months, years) of despair. Ben N. (T-358) told of a close friend who went to the wires (i.e., electrocuted himself on the fence) and how sorely tempted he was to follow. Still another told about how he was about to throw himself in front of a train when a friend whom he hadn't seen in ages recognized him. Daniel F. (T-978) decided it was not his time. Daniel was and remains conventionally religious. The same holds true for Ben N.[3]

If witnesses did not live in a world in which their suffering was filled with meaning, neither do they currently (i.e., at the time of the interview) live in a world in which their souls have been destroyed, as Levi puts it. Most have managed to partition off that obliterated portion of themselves in order to go on living – not with their souls intact, in most cases, but with a goodly portion of soul remaining. They have not been restored as Job was – a state I question, in any case – but neither have they been destroyed. To be sure, most survivors experience absurdity, not affliction, due in no small measure to the experience of Auschwitz itself. This includes Levi. The rebellion that was open to Albert Camus's (1955) Sisyphus – who rebels against the absurd task the gods place before him and so finds meaning, indeed, happiness in his struggle – is but a cruel philosophical joke when applied to survivors. The refusal to submit that is the glory of

---

3 Interviews based on my research in the Fortunoff Archives are identifiable in the text by the prefix "T-" followed by the accession number. In each case, the full citation should read: _____ [first name and last initial of witness] (T-XXXX), Fortunoff Video Archives for Holocaust Testimonies, Yale University Library.

Sisyphus becomes not merely survival but also surviving survival, for most witnesses. For a human being, that is sometimes enough.

The second reason I turn to Job is that Levi (2002, 3–21) places Job at the beginning of his own work, seeing Job not merely as one who suffers unjustly but also as one who stands for the meaninglessness of human suffering. Levi cannot imagine a God who would so afflict Job. In understanding Levi's interpretation of Job, it becomes possible to understand a little more clearly Levi's own position on God and suffering in this world. It is not quite as obvious as it might seem.

Finally, I take seriously the questions raised by the Book of Job because I take seriously the question of God. Not the literal question of whether He exists; to feel compelled to answer that question is to already have missed the point. How could humans know such things for sure? Are humans not hubristic to make such assertions as starting points? Better to let long and careful study lead us to the realization that one does not have to answer that question to take God seriously.

Raymond Scheindlin (1998), translator of a recent version of the Book of Job, suggests that Job was right all along, which means that God was wrong. God tormented Job for no good reason. How can humans live with such knowledge? Not by any information conveyed by the poem but rather by the rhythmic experience of the poem itself. "Job's poetry achieves the book's purpose of consolation partly by providing its own vigor as an antidote to its pessimism" (1998, 25). Scheindlin's argument is not so different from that of Friedrich Nietzsche's in *The Birth of Tragedy out of the Spirit of Music*.[4]

Yet, we must be careful not to accept Scheindlin's attractive answer too quickly. The theology of the Book of Job is more complex than he allows. The authors of the Book of Job appear to be making a distinction between internal and external piety, telling us that Job was indeed tested and found wanting (i.e., God was not wrong; Job was not right). Although Job finds it easy enough to tell his wife that if we accept the good from God, we must also accept the bad, it is not a lesson he can live with himself for more than a week. Soon enough, Job wants to take God to court. We learn, in other words, that Job only appeared to be God's humble servant. In reality, Job was filled

---

[4] This is the original title of the 1872 edition. In 1886, Nietzsche changed the title to *The Birth of Tragedy, Or: Hellenism and Pessimism* (1968b).

with pride – indeed, hubris – imagining that he could put God on the witness stand almost as though God were another earthly power. Finally confronted by the Lord of the whirlwind, Job learns that God belongs to another dimension of being. Job learns that his fantasy about taking Yahweh to court made about as much sense as putting the universe on trial. Job learns a lesson that is in some respects beyond words, for he has been confronted by God, who has laid out His universe before him. Job lived – not lived to tell about it, just lived.

Levi must tell about his experiences. He could not help himself. "I returned from the camp with an absolute, pathological narrative charge," he stated (Anissimov 2000, 257). Following his theophany, Job says not a word about his experiences, which at least in one respect resembles that of survivors. Job also loses his first family but gains a second. What we never learn from Job is whether the loss of his first family spoils in some way the tender love he feels for his second, whether Job lives a double life with his second family – his murdered first family hovering in the background. Certainly, some survivors feel the loss of their first family most intensely while in the midst of their second. Levi lost not a single member of his family to the Nazis.

Clarification of the Terms of Discourse and Statement of My Thesis

Affliction is not merely suffering extended over time. Affliction is suffering experienced as meaningful. Weil's explication is paradigmatic, although anyone who emerges enriched from an experience of suffering has experienced affliction. The person need not believe, and often doesn't, that the education was worth the price.

Absurd suffering – suffering that seems meaningless, purposeless, pointless – is the problem. Sometimes pointlessness stems from the innocence of the victim, sometimes from the magnitude of the pain and loss either personally or because of the numbers of victims involved. Sometimes the world itself is rendered meaningless because one cannot imagine a sensible world in which terrible suffering has no point at all.

To some degree, we must accept the last possibility. Dumb, brute suffering is the lot of most men and women at most times and places, including our own. We should not work too hard to transform all suffering into affliction, as though doing so were a moral duty, as though the failure to do so were a sign of moral or psychological weakness. "Suffering happens," variant of a cruder motto, makes as much sense of this world as any other, at least at first glance. Suffering is meaningful when it is meaningful. We cannot and should not force it to be so, although we can and should work hard to make the conditions of collective life less absurd, more meaningful. Reform of the material, moral, and spiritual conditions of everyday life is all important in this regard.

My thesis is that absurd suffering is on the rise, especially since Auschwitz. The mark of modernity, absurd suffering started long before Auschwitz and continues for reasons having little to do with Auschwitz. Nevertheless, Auschwitz is the high-water mark of absurd suffering, and from studying it there we can learn much.

Job's Abjection

Covered in sores from the crown of his head to the soles of his feet, Job represents the breakdown of the body when it is exposed to the universe, separated from the protection of God (Job 2:7–8). The abject, said Kristeva, represents life in a particularly intensified form: life on the edge of death, separated from all that normally supports us – from the law to the routines of everyday life. The abject concerns "what disturbs identity, system, order. What does not respect borders, positions, rules" (Kristeva 1982, 4).

Job's abjection, it is apparent, only begins with his physical state. It has ultimately to do with the inexplicability of his suffering, the breakdown of what is called *Deuteronomic theology* (c. 28), the theology of his friends Eliphaz, Bildad, and Zophar. According to Deuteronomic theology, God keeps the world in moral balance, rewarding the good and punishing the bad. By the end of the Book of Job, God Himself will reject this theology, suggesting that were Job himself not present to intervene on behalf of his friends, then God might well sacrifice them (42:7–8). Why? Because they have not learned the lesson of Job's suffering: God is not subject to our ideas of Him.

Because abjection is the breakdown of the symbolic order, represented by the body, the figurative equation *body* = *world* becomes an identity. Given the presymbolic character of the reasoning involved, body does not so much represent the world as become the world.

The realm of the symbolic is impoverished, as the ego is drawn to the Siren's terrifying call of nonbeing, the self undifferentiated from its world. More precisely, body becomes an abjected, cast-off piece of the world. Think of Job, sitting among the dust and ashes, scraping his sores with a shard of pottery, more dead than alive (2:7–8) – or so it seems for a moment, until Job breaks his silence and begins to curse the day of his birth. Soon, Job will lament God's injustice and not long after that, Job will express his not-so-secret desire: to take God to court.

In doing these things, Job will have found abjection's apparent solution: the creation of a new symbolic order under which categories of justice and law, underpinned by rage (as perhaps they always are; this seems to be the lesson of Aeschylus' *Eumenides*), reign supreme. Under this new regime, sign, rule, and norm create borders, positions, boundaries, and rules. This is the order Job is attempting to restore when he longs to take God to court, the realm in which law rules. If this were not absurd, then the symbolic order would be restored and so would Job's identity as an autonomous individual, master of his destiny – at least, in comparison with the abjection that has been inflicted on him.

Beginning with the appearance of Elihu (32:1), the remainder of the Book of Job is concerned with God's true nature (which is not subject to the law) and the way in which Job is shown to have failed to understand not just God but also his own nature and place in the world. One wants to say that Job is released from his abjection. In fact, he is introduced to a new dimension of abjection – and so are we, the readers.

Abjection in literature (i.e., in art, as opposed to in life) is roughly comparable in its effect to the experience of the sublime. Immanuel Kant (1987, sec. 23–7) wrote of the sublime as an insult to the imagination. So awesome is the experience that we are unprepared for it even in our imagination.[5] Simply stated, the sublime is an uncontainable moment of excess, and it is this aspect that postmoderns, including Kristeva, have found so fruitful.

In the experience of the sublime, we are protected from the abject only by being immersed in it, the abject wrapped in the cocoon of

---

[5] We are unprepared even if, as always for Kant, we create the possibility of this experience through our imposition of categories on the world.

beauty (Kristeva 1982, 29). Stated a little too simply, beauty is the difference between reading Sartre's *Nausea* and being its protagonist, Antoine Roquentin; between being Job and reading the Book of Job. Kristeva, however, would not draw quite so sharply the distinction between being Job and reading about Job. For Kristeva, the only experience of Job that matters is the literary experience we the readers have of the Book of Job:

> On close inspection, all literature is probably a version of the apocalypse that seems to me rooted, no matter what its sociohistorical conditions might be, on the fragile border (borderline cases) where identities (subject/object, etc.) do not exist or only barely so – double, fuzzy, heterogeneous, animal, metamorphosed, altered, abject. (Kristeva 1982, 207)

In a literal sense, Kristeva is quite right; Job doesn't exist, probably never did, and his actual subjectivity (as distinct from the subjectivity of Job the character in the Book of Job) is unknowable to us. Nevertheless, it will sometimes be useful to distinguish between Job the character in the Book of Job and the reader's experience of the Book of Job.

That Job epitomizes abjection is easy enough to establish. What is not quite so clear is that God's appearance in the whirlwind does nothing to lift Job out of his abjection. On the contrary, theophany only confirms Job's abjection in another dimension. One cannot say this dimension is the realm of art, for only the reader can experience the Book of Job as art. Nevertheless, God Himself introduces Job to the world as an experience of the sublime. In that sense, God represents the world to Job as art – or, perhaps we should say, as a sacred, numinous experience.

In fact, God's representation of the world to Job is neither religion nor art. God presents Job with the awesome, awful, unadulterated magnificence of the natural order that He, God, has created. In the face of such an order (and it is an order but on a scale Job never imagined), Job is overwhelmed. He experiences a second abjection in the realm of nature as experience of the sublime. Once again, Job's categories are shattered; except this time, Job does not seek refuge in the familiar symbolic order, perhaps because he is already "living in the position of the dead," as in the Japanese expression (Benedict 1946, 248–50). The phrase refers to one who has suffered a terrible experience of shame and humiliation, resulting in the loss of any claim on society's respect and, therefore, any place in the moral hierarchy. Some Japanese kill themselves and so become truly dead. A few experience a profound sense of liberation because they have nothing left to lose, no status to maintain. To lose one's earthly standing is to be set free.

Free to what? In Job's case, freedom means the freedom to live within the space of his abjection. This Job has learned from his encounter with God how to live in a world that "was not made for the sake of the human being, and . . . has not become more human," as Herbert Marcuse (1978, 69) lamented in his last book. One might be tempted to assimilate abjection to what Camus called the absurd, which would be a mistake. With the term *absurd*, Camus (1955, 28) referred to the confrontation between the human need for meaning and the world's unreasoning silence ("*L'absurde naît de cette confrontation entre l'appel humain et le silence déraisonnable du monde*" [Camus 1942, 45]). Camus used the term *confrontation* not because every encounter with the absurd results in a rebellion against it but rather because rebellion against absurdity always remains a possibility (Camus 1955).

One does not rebel against abjection. The concept makes no sense. One lives in the space of abjection. If one is fortunate, as Job is, one is able to make this space sacred, which means to render it once again symbolic albeit in a new way. Kristeva (1984, 21–106) described this process in terms of the distinction between the symbolic and semiotic elements of signification.[6] The symbolic refers to what philosophers might think of as meaning per se, conveyed by the grammar of symbols. The semiotic element is the prelinguistic, body-based experience of the drives (Kristeva 1984, 25–30).[7] Without the symbolic element of signification, there would be only sounds and psychotic babble. Without the semiotic element, signification would be empty, lacking

[6] Kristeva's is a much more precise use of the term *symbolic* than that of Jacques Lacan, for whom the *symbolic* refers to signification in its broadest sense, including culture in general (Oliver 2002, xv). Kristeva's *symbolic* is a technical term that refers to one element of language, most especially that having to do with syntax. Neither should Kristeva's semiotic element (*le sémiotique*) be confused with semiotics (*la sémiotique*), the science of signs.

[7] Kristeva calls this prelinguistic space the semiotic *chora*, drawing on Plato's term, which is often translated as *womb* or *receptacle* (Plato, *The Timaeus* 52b–53a; Kristeva 1984, 25–30).

vitality, lacking Eros – the feeling that one's words are not empty but rather are filled with the rhythms of life. Simply stated, we have a bodily need to communicate the realm of the semiotic; the symbolic provides the structure necessary to do so (Kristeva 1984, 21–106).

Whereas Levi is able to transform his suffering into narrative, the authors of the Book of Job are able to transform his suffering into sacred narrative, an effect indicative of the intensity with which the symbolic is invested with the semiotic. Job says it this way in the dramatic climax of the Book:

> I knew You, but only by rumor;
> My eye has beheld You today.
> I retract. I even take comfort
> in dust and ashes. (42:5–6)

In taking comfort in dust and ashes, Job is taking comfort in the symbols of mortality and death, as well as the symbols of mourning – symbols that Job is finally able to use to express much the same point as Marcuse. Not the Marcuse of *Eros and Civilization* who longed for Nirvana but rather the Marcuse (1978, 69) who wrote in his last book of his disappointment in a nature with which humans have not become reconciled. The difference is that Job is able to take comfort in his mortality – indeed, in his personal insignificance in the order of things. For Job knows there is an order – *"Hier gibt es ein warum"* ("Here there is a why, a reason") – even if he does not know what it is. Job has moved from abjection to affliction.

Levi made a similar journey but, unlike Job's, Levi's journey was endangered at almost every turn by the possibility that his experience might become merely absurd. Absurd experience does not lack semiotic content. Absurdity is a higher-level disorder, so to speak, in which the syntax of symbolism is disturbed. Eugène Ionesco's *The Bald Soprano* (2007) and T. S. Elliot's *The Cocktail Party* (1950) exemplify the absurd, in each case by means of the decontextualization of ordinary language. The same thing occurs, on a much grander and more perverted scale, when a camp guard replied to Levi's question *"Warum?"* that *"Hier gibt es kein warum."* The *result* is a withdrawal of affect (roughly equivalent to the semiotic element of language), but this seems to stem from the lack of symbolic meaning rather than being its cause.

In the case of survivors, it will be argued that they are forced into doubling because the world of Auschwitz is absurd: not devoid of meaning but rather devoid of a meaning compatible with ordinary life. Life in and after Auschwitz comes to be experienced as death. In the absence of doubling, the survivor could not survive. One of the simplest statements about Levi is that he was finally overwhelmed by Auschwitz because he did not double enough. Or, rather, he let his books and essays do his doubling for him. "My books," he said, have "interposed themselves, in a curious way, like an artificial memory, but also like a defensive barrier, between my very normal present and the dramatic past" (Levi 1995, 230). Why Levi's way of doubling, so creative in many respects, might also be particularly dangerous for his soul is discussed in Chapter 4.

Job's World

Because he was a righteous and upright man, Job had been richly rewarded by God. Job had many flocks, many children, and many servants. Yet, in only a matter of days, his flocks are destroyed by lightning or stolen by thieves, and his adult children are crushed to death by a mighty wind that collapses a building in which they have come together to feast. In each case, only one servant survives to tell the tale. Job has lost all. Only his wife remains, Mrs. Job, whose name was later said to be Sitis.

Job is devastated, as one might expect, and yet he does not curse or blaspheme God. On the contrary, he says simply, "Should we accept the good from God and not accept the bad?" (1:20). God is impressed. Not only has God been watching all that has befallen Job with great interest; God has allowed it to take place. Indeed, this is what makes the Book of Job unique. The problem addressed by Job, the suffering of the innocent and good, had been around since long before the Book of Job was written. (The Book of Job was almost surely written between the reign of Solomon [circa 900 BCE] and the postexilic period [fifth century BCE]; likely it was composed over several centuries because it is heavily redacted. The dramatic date of the Book of Job is between 2000 BCE and 1000 BCE.) Premonotheistic creation myths, such as those known to us from Ugaritic and Babylonian literature, refer to the situation of a man like Job (Scheindlin 1998, 11).

What is unique about the Book of Job is the opening frame scene, the way it lets us in on the negotiations between God and Satan so that we, the readers – like the audience in a Greek tragedy – know the character of the gods and the plans they have for the protagonists. However, putting it this way isn't quite right and not only because Satan isn't a god. Satan isn't even Satan yet – that is, an independent power in his own right, a fallen angel. At this earlier stage in Biblical theology, Satan is still one of God's minions, doing God's work – God's tester, he might be called. It might seem as though Satan were working freelance, and perhaps that is his desire; but, it is clear that the Lord is in command, setting the limits beyond which the Satan cannot go.

What is the Satan testing? One wants to say that Satan is helping God and us (for let us not forget that we are reading a text written by human authors for human readers) to distinguish between external and internal or actual piety. Seen from this perspective, it turns out that Satan's charge against Job is true, albeit with emendation. Job fails not so much because his piety depends on being richly rewarded by God. Job fails because he has come to believe that he deserves to be richly rewarded because he is, in fact, pious and upright. Job was tested and found wanting. This is not the whole story, but it is a start.

Job has lost his possessions and his children, and still he does not curse God. So, Satan turns to God and says, in effect, double or nothing. "Skin for skin" is how some translations interpret it, evidently an ancient expression. Satan suspects that Job never really cared for his possessions or his family in the first place. That too was a bluff; but, if you torment him in his body, he will curse you to your face. Once again, God takes Satan up on his bet, even as the reader remains uneasy about a God who is so easily goaded into making bets with the Satan. "Afflict Job's body in any way you please," the Satan is instructed by the Lord. "Only you may not kill him." Instantly, it seems, Job is covered with loathsome sores from the crown of his head to the soles of his feet. Job is reduced to sitting on an ash heap, scraping himself with a broken shard of pottery, having lost everything.

Once again, his wife approaches, and this time she speaks – her only lines: "Are you still persisting in your innocence? Curse God and die!" (2:9).[8] To this encouraging effort of spousal support, their only exchange, Job responds by calling her a foolish woman and repeats, "Should we accept the good from God and not accept the bad?" (2:10). About this exchange the narrator says, "In spite of everything, Job did not sin with his lips." One is left to wonder about Job's thoughts.

The Book continues. Job's three friends, Eliphaz, Bildad, and Zophar, come to commiserate, and the first thing they do is the greatest. They sit silently with Job for a week, saying nothing, sharing in his suffering. After a week, Job's friends begin to talk – and if they got it exactly right the first week, they got it exactly wrong the second.

Consider this admittedly loose and imprecise contemporary parallel. Your friend has just lost virtually his entire family to a terrible car crash. Not only that, but about a year before, he was diagnosed with cancer. As you greet your friend at the funeral home with the appropriate solemn looks and supportive comments, you grip him solidly on his shoulder. The next day you go by his house and the day after that too. You don't say much, but you touch him on the arms and shoulders a lot, mostly to let him know that you are there and that you care.

A few days later, you find yourself at your bereaved friend's bedside at the hospital, where he has been admitted. As you stand over his bed, you say something like the following: "You know, Joe, it was really your own fault that your family died and that you are no longer in remission. You did not lead a blameless and upright life; you did not lead your children in the paths of righteousness; you set a bad example. No wonder God took them from you. Probably that's why your cancer has returned."

That is not what your friend needs to hear at this point. That is not what good friends say to each other in times of grief and woe. Of course, that's not quite what Eliphaz, Zophar, and Bildad said. They couched their criticisms of Job in Deuteronomic theology, in which sins of the children – as well as the unknowing and unwitting sins of Job himself – might have brought doom on Job. However, that distinction

---

[8] The Hebrew here and at 1:5 for "curse God" employs a euphemism, literally "bless God." Some read Satan as using Mrs. Job to tempt Job as Eve tempted Adam, provoking God to administer the final punishment.

is an accident of history. The basic principle remains the same. Job is responsible for his fate because the principle of Deuteronomic theology (Deuteronomy 28) rules: good things happen to good people; bad things happen to bad people. God rewards the upright and punishes the wicked. If terrible things happen to you, then it is a sign that you have sinned.

Why do Job's friends talk this way? Not, presumably, because they are harsh and uncaring but rather because without this principle, the world would not make sense. They would be unable to find order in God's world. The world would be unknowable, absurd, without an ordering principle – or, at least, without a straightforward principle that simple prophets like them could divine.

Job's patience is at an end – the legendary patience of Job having lasted about a week. Whereas Job's three friends have contributed to his anger, it is God Himself who is the target of Job's rage. Not just rage; Job's rage borders on heresy, although perhaps that puts it too mildly.[9] What Job says is heresy, except that because the dramatic date is some time before 1000 BCE, and Job is a gentile, it is difficult to say which doctrine exists. Without doctrine, there can be no heresy. However, whichever doctrine Job holds to (and likely it is almost identical to that of the Jewish authors of the text), surely it is heresy to claim that:

> God destroys the blameless and the wicked alike. (9:22)
> God mocks the despair of the innocent. (9:23)
> God would crush me for no reason but because he is strong and I am not; he would multiply my wounds for no good reason but to display his power. (9:19)

---

[9] Virtually all commentators point out that Job does not commit blasphemy. True enough, but these same commentators generally assume that it is blasphemy, not heresy, that is at issue. It will pay to distinguish them. *Heresy* is theological or religious opinion or doctrine maintained in opposition or held to be contrary to orthodox doctrine. *Blasphemy* is the defamation of God or gods and, by extension, gross irreverence toward any person or thing worthy of worship. *Sacrilege* means to profane sacred things, such as snacking on communion wafers. It is difficult to see where Job commits blasphemy at any point. Job does seem to commit heresy, except that the events take place so far in the past, outside any organized religion (Job is neither Jewish nor pagan), that it is difficult to know what counts as orthodox opinion and, hence, as heresy. Still, to say as Job does that God enjoys watching the righteous suffer and die before their time while the guilty go on to live long and happy lives (9:19–24) must be heresy to any righteous man, including Job, who seems to worship the same God as the Jews.

God arranges it so that judges convict the innocent, and free the guilty.
(9:24)
I know that God has wronged me. Though I cry for help, there is no
justice. (19:6)

Add to this Job's first curse: not that he should never have been
born but rather that the day he was born should never have existed
(3:3–7). An arrogant, hubristic, reverse Genesis is present here. If my
life is hell, then the day I was born should not exist for anyone.

Yet, this is not all that Job has to say about God. The line made
famous by Handel, "I know that my redeemer liveth" (19:25), also
comes from Job. Whereas it is a Christian bad habit to read Jesus
Christ back into Job (and now we see that not only is it a bad habit, it
is bad theology as well), Job indeed wants to love and be cared for by
the God who torments him. One thinks here of nothing so much as
an abused child, wanting to be loved and protected by the parent who
abuses him, having to split the parent (and, ultimately, his own fragile
psyche) in two to do so.

Lest the reader think I am psychologizing Job (just wait until Chapter 2), it is well to quote a nonpsychological reading, that of Gustavo
Gutiérrez, *On Job: God-Talk and the Suffering of the Innocent* (2003):

It might almost be said that Job, as it were, splits God in two and produces a
God who is judge and a God who will defend him at that supreme moment;
a God whom he experiences as almost an enemy but whom he knows at the
same time to be truly a friend. He has just now accused God of persecuting
him, but at the same time he knows that God is just and does not want human
beings to suffer. . . . At an earlier point, but in a less trenchant way, Job had
already appealed to God against God. "If only you would keep me safe in the
abyss and shelter me there till your anger is past and you appoint a place
for reconciliation with me!" [14:13]. God could protect Job against God and
God's anger by hiding him in Sheol, which is a kind of nonworld within the
world. (65)

My argument is almost the same except that I do not start with the
assumption that God must be just, that He must truly be a friend. This
assumption about their parents is what drives young children who
are abused crazy, leading them to split not just their parents but also
themselves. It could drive a young Job crazy.

But it doesn't. For Job is in the grips of a fantasy, one that will save
him for a little while until he can know the truth. What is Job's fantasy?

That he can put God on trial, that God will take the witness stand and answer Job's charges against Him under rules of law. It is the last thing Job says before Elihu speaks and Yahweh makes his appearance in the whirlwind:

> Here is my desire: that Shaddai answer me,
> That my opponent write a brief. (31:35)

Over and over, Job imagines what it would be like to put God on the witness stand: "I want to dispute with El" (13:3). Over and over, Job imagines what he would say to Him if they were – if not equal – at least equal before the law, as we say today:

> For a man like me cannot just challenge Him,
> "Let's go to court together!"
> Now if there were an arbiter between us
> To lay his hand on both of us,
> To make Him take His rod away,
> So that His terror would not cow me,
> Then I could speak without this fear of Him;
> For now I am not steady in his presence. (9:32–35)

The result, of course, is only to heighten the irony of the Book of Job. For when God finally utters His famous words from the whirlwind, "Where were you when I laid the foundations of the earth? Speak if you have understanding," we understand that Job (and we) are confronting a different order of being – one closer to infinity, an order of being that encompasses nonbeing as well – if that is even comprehensible.

Like the whirlwind itself, once set in motion, God does not readily come to rest. He asks Job a long series of sarcastic, rhetorical questions, along the lines of "Where were you when I created the heavens, set the constellations in motion, separated the land from the waters, gave the dawn its orders, gave the stallion its strength?" Inhuman in His power, surprisingly human in His sarcasm and pride of workmanship, God is both a character and beyond all human characterization. Job was a fool to believe that he could put God on trial, rather as if he could put the universe on trial. Indeed, one might almost say that God is not so much master of the universe as He *is* the universe.

Surprise to say, Job gets it. He understands that he had it completely wrong about God, that he has confronted a different order of existence and lived – not lived to tell about it, just lived. Furthermore, God is not particularly angry with Job and his heresies but rather with Job's friends, who think they know. "For you have not spoken rightly about me as did my servant Job" (42:7). Perhaps Job was not mistaken in his rage; his rage was simply irrelevant, like that of a little child against the world.

The Book concludes (42:7–16) with an addition by still later and more literal-minded redactors – or, at least, later redactors for the more literal-minded – in which Job is given a new and better family, with daughters even more beautiful than before, as well as bigger flocks. That this is a late addition virtually no scholars disagree. The real end of the Book, or so it seems, returns to where Job's sufferings began: Job taking comfort in his dust and ashes, for that is what he is and all that he has, all that any human can be (42:6) – merely mortal.

Job has come to a completely new realization of how he stands in relationship to God (42:5–6). His affliction has taught him a lesson, the lesson he would teach his wife but could not believe himself: that one accepts all things from God – and, hence, all things – in a spirit of wonder, mystery, and resignation.

If we wonder why Job was afflicted, then we have already missed the point. If instead we say to ourselves something like the authors of the Book of Job might have said to themselves, then we get it: "God is great. He exists, acts, and plans on a scale humans can't even imagine (Isaiah 55:8). So, questions like 'Why do good people suffer?' do not have an answer, at least no more of an answer than the question, 'Why does the universe exist?' Or, rather, in each case the answer is the same: because it is God's will, which humans are unlikely to ever understand but must choose to faithfully accept if we are to live in harmony with the Ruler of the Universe."

Some Problems in Translating the Book of Job

The Book of Job is one of the more difficult books of the Bible to translate, in part due to the richness of its vocabulary. (In a passage devoted to starving lions, 4:10–11, five different words for *lion* are used.) One might argue that the text employs many rare and obscure words, but this may be because the meanings of many words were forgotten when Hebrew ceased to be a spoken language in the first or second century of the Common Era (CE) (Scheindlin 1998, 28–9). This has led some to argue that the Book was intentionally couched in a difficult language by its authors to obscure its unorthodox ideas. Although this is possible, some of Job's harshest criticisms against God are written in "lucid basic Hebrew, intelligible to this day to any Hebrew-speaking schoolchild" (Scheindlin 1998, 31).

The problem is not so much the obscurity of the text as it is the multiple meanings or interpretations that are possible, many of which are contradictory. Consider, for example, the well-known line from the King James translation, "Though He slay me, yet I will trust Him" (13:15).

- The Revised Standard Version (RSV) reads, "Behold He will slay me, I have no hope."
- The Anchor Bible reads, "He may slay me, I'll not quaver."
- The New English Bible reads, "If He wishes to slay me, I have nothing to lose."

Only the King James Version unambiguously supports the view of Job as more pious than pious, saying, in effect, "Do with me what you want, God, prove to me that you are not righteous as humans understand the term, and I still will believe in you." Other versions suggest a quite different Job.

In fact, the translation problem is even worse than that. For one could readily read, "Though He slay me, yet I will trust Him" as "Though He slay me, yet I will *not* trust Him." One can *hear* the ancient Hebrew either way. Tradition, usually referred to as the Masoretic text, renders the text the first way for fairly obvious reasons of faith. The term *Mesorah* refers to the diacritical markings of the text of the Tanakh (The Hebrew Bible) and marginal comments regarding the division of words and the like that were made by a group of Jews known as the Masoretes between the seventh and tenth centuries CE. This is how they heard the text, this is how they transmitted it; however, what the original authors and editors really meant, we have not a clue – or, rather, we have too many clues, mixed with our own longings and intuitions. Ordinarily, one would turn to context to settle issues like this, but when it is the context that is in question, then almost every passage can seem unsettled.[10]

Consider the last lines of the poem (not the text) as it is rendered in the RSV: "Therefore I despise myself and repent in dust and ashes" (42:6). In the Hebrew, the term translated as "despise" has no object, which is a product of the translation, one not unique to the RSV. However, consider the possibility that Job might despise, regret, or abhor his situation, or the situation of the world in which he has found himself, or even the nature of the God about whom he has learned: a God who has little care to offer humans and even less justice.[11] If the latter interpretation seems a stretch, it is worth noting that it fits perfectly with Scheindlin's (1998, 22–6) introduction to his translation of the Book of Job, in which he wrote that Job has resigned himself to the lot of being merely human and the terrible losses that go with it. Job regrets the dust and ashes of human mortality more than ever, for it is uncompensated by the care or justice of God – at least, not in a manner humans can comprehend.

What are those of us who are not Hebraists to make of all this? A great deal of intellectual modesty – indeed, humbleness – would seem to be in order. Still, the Bible was written for all of us and, if fools rush in . . . let us at least tread lightly. These considerations explain, however, why I employ several translations and why fidelity to any particular translation is no unalloyed virtue. All translations are a long way from home; all are but a woven web of educated guesses.

In the end, perhaps it is not so important to divine the original intent as it is to use (carefully) texts such as the Book of Job to speak with each other about those issues that, humans being who they are, will never go away – issues such as the meaning of suffering. For the danger in the contemporary world seems to be not so much that the Book of Job will be carelessly misread as that the issues it raises will be forgotten, as men and women invent new and ever more one-dimensional ways in which to understand themselves. Suffering as a biochemical imbalance seems to be a particularly popular, and empty, account – at least, in the contemporary industrialized world.

---

[10] Professor Aryeh Botwinick helped me with these and other problems in translation.
[11] This is from a lecture by Professor Amy-Jill Levine of Vanderbilt Divinity School.

Plan of the Text

Chapter 2 focuses on the Book of Job, characterizing his journey from abjection to affliction and asking what is required for a person to make this passage. After answering this question, the chapter psychoanalyzes the character God (actually, Yahweh) in the text called the Book of Job. This may seem more than a little arrogant, and I beg the readers' forgiveness, asking them to remember that the context here is one of reading the Book of Job as a literary text. (I do not believe that it matters whether one regards the Book of Job as a sacred text; no less a devout reader than G. K. Chesterton [1916] regarded God as the only real character, other than Job, in the Old Testament.) The question raised is why God might treat Job so ruthlessly. The answer, I suggest, is so that God might learn what manner of being He has created. Is this man Job, benighted everyman, one who can stand on his own two feet, continuing to practice piety and right living even as God steps back from His creation?

Chapter 3 introduces the testimony of a number of survivors of the Holocaust. What does it mean, I ask, to live after having died at Auschwitz, as so many say they did? What does it mean to live a double life, the leading explanation employed by survivors themselves to make sense of how they manage to live apparently normal lives? In making sense of survivors' experiences, I draw on the work of Kristeva as well as the work of several cognitive psychologists. The goal, however, is not, in the end, to interpret survivors. It is to listen to survivors to understand better what they have to teach us. After listening to hours and hours of testimony, my thoughts kept turning to the perpetrators. Why would humans design such a system of torment, torture, degradation, and death? Interpreting survivors should not be an end in itself. We should seek to understand survivors better in order to learn from them terrible truths about the world that only they can teach us, truths that unavoidably center on the cruelty of the human heart. The teachings of survivors are a dark teaching, but what else is the Holocaust?

Chapter 3 makes only sporadic attempts to connect the suffering of survivors to that of Job. In some ways, the most obvious connection is a disconnection. The experience of transcendence available to Job was lost in the absurdity of the Holocaust, never to be found again. This argument is developed in the following two chapters. Fortunately, it is not nearly as simple as this one sentence suggests.

Chapter 4 addresses the work of Primo Levi. For many, Levi was the man who kept his humanity through the most dreadful circumstances, thereby restoring our confidence in humankind. For many, Levi's suicide seemed to devalue all that he had taught us. Only in the years since his death is it possible to see his work as a whole, to see that he was always struggling with a darker question – a question closer to the one raised in previous chapters: how to keep not just his suffering but also human suffering from remaining stuck in the realm of the absurd, the haunting ground of abjection. Chapter 4 concludes with a discussion of the absurd, suggesting that the category of surplus absurdity – loosely modeled on Marcuse's concept of surplus repression – might help make sense of experiences such as Auschwitz.

Chapter 5 continues the discussion of surplus absurdity, arguing that it is best transcended by paying attention to particulars. The question this approach raises, of course, is whether paying attention to particulars has anything to do with transcendence. Is it not instead the idealization of immanence? In arguing that it is not – or, at least, that it is not so simple – I dispute with Gilles Deleuze, theorist of pure immanence. The chapter continues with the leading themes of this book: asking whether Primo Levi was the simple atheist he seemed to be, taking up once again his struggle with the Book of Job. The chapter concludes by asking what survivors have to teach us about the world, not just themselves. Could survivors teach us to look at the Holocaust in such a way as to render it less absurd?

One theme that unites these chapters is, of course, the relationship among suffering, absurdity, and affliction. Another is interpretation. In substantial parts of two chapters – perhaps the most unlikely parts of the most unlikely chapters – an interpretation influenced by psychoanalysis is employed: the interpretation of God's relationship to Job, as mentioned previously, and the interpretation of aspects of survivor testimony. Anyone who approaches the testimony of survivors of the Holocaust from a psychoanalytic perspective, as I do in parts of Chapter 3, does so at his or her moral peril. I refer not only to the legacy of Bruno Bettelheim's (1943) psychoanalytic interpretation

of concentration-camp inmates' tendency to identify with their tormentors and generally engage in regressive behavior, an interpretation that does little to conceal an attitude of contempt toward his
fellow survivors.[12] The moral peril also stems from applying psychoanalytic categories appropriate to everyday life to extreme situations.
The moral peril stems from analyzing what one does not understand,
cannot fully understand, unless one was there. Above all, the moral
peril stems from the arrogance of analyzing a survivor who has gone
through hell when one should be mightily struggling simply to understand.

The work of psychoanalysts such as Kristeva as well as that of cognitive psychologists such as Robert Kraft (2002) directs us toward the
experience of horror and thus leads us to ask not merely, "What happened to the witness?" but also, "Why in the world would humans
inflict such horror on others?" In other words, choosing the right psychoanalyst is important because on this choice rests the question of
whether we remain focused on the victims or turn to the terrorism
of the perpetrators. If one thinks about psychoanalysis as the legacy of
Freud, then it is the Freud of *Civilization and Its Discontents* (1930) and
Totem and Taboo (1912), not the Freud of *The Interpretation of Dreams*
(1900), with which I am concerned. Influential here is the legacy
of Freud the social theorist, Freud the theorist of the *Todestrieb* (i.e.,
death drive), not Freud the theorist of individual neurosis – although
doubtless they are related.

Chapter 4 about Levi relies heavily on interpretation of a much
more eclectic variety in which I seek to understand Primo Levi the
man while remaining aware that his writing was as much an attempt
to conceal as to reveal the author. About Levi, it is often held that the
narrator and the man were virtually one. One critic called Levi (of all
things) "the Nick Carraway of Turin" to capture Levi's straightforward
simplicity of style and thought. Only later did she come to see the

---

[12] For an example of a disparaging interpretation, consider this: "Prisoners seemed,
for instance, particularly sensitive to punishments similar to those which a parent
might inflict on his child. . . . So they reacted to it not as an adult, but in a childish
way – with embarrassment and shame, with violent, impotent, and unmanageable
emotions directed, not against the system, but against the person inflicting the
punishment" (Bettelheim 1946, para. 25).

irony of that designation. Nick Carraway is a fictional narrator, entirely unlike his creator, F. Scott Fitzgerald (Simpson 2007). We may say much the same about the man Primo Levi and the narrator of his books. However, with Levi, a little interpretation goes a long way, and it is neither possible nor desirable to do more than to try to disentangle the man and the narrator.

2

Job, Transitional Space, and the Ruthless Use of the Object

The usual psychoanalytic approach to religion has changed from an analysis of the defensive psychological function of religious belief – Freud's approach – to an analysis of the transference. For Freud, particularly in *Totem and Taboo* (1912), religion is an obsessional neurosis, an attempt to ward off guilt by repetition. Guilt stems from the primal horde's killing of the father, an event reproduced in every boy's oedipal struggle with his own father. Religion is the obsessive repetition of the ritualized reconciliation with an idealized patriarchal father god. "By rooting religion in the instinctual life of the child, Freud offered a biological hermeneutic of the sacred" (Jones 1991, 2).

In his later work, *The Future of an Illusion* (1927), Freud understood religion in both less reductive and less speculative terms. Religion reduces the terror of an uncaring nature by personalizing the natural order. Religion removes the fear of death by providing the illusion of immortality. Above all, religion reconciles us to the self-denial required by civilization by promising an infinite happiness in the hereafter. In this work, Freud was confident that the future would bring with it a weakening of the need for religious illusion. Piety would be abandoned and morality assumed. Noble sentiments, indeed, but difficult to reconcile with the dark vision of *Civilization and Its Discontents* (1930), which was published only three years later.

Remarkable is how little of Freud's account of religion fits Job. Most of the Book of Job concerns Job's heretical rage at "his Father who art in heaven," as the King James Version of the Bible almost puts it

(Mt 6:9). Furthermore, Job has no illusions about immortality. Beginning before the dramatic date at which the Book of Job is set, about 1000 BCE, and continuing to the probable date of composition, Sheol was both heaven and hell – or, rather, Sheol is neither, a netherworld so disordered and dreadful that "even the light is like darkness" (10:22).[1] Finally, what Job learns from God is that His universe has nothing to do with Job's security, welfare, or happiness. Yet, somehow Job is comforted by this hard-won knowledge, gained in his journey from hubris to abjection to the wisdom of abjection. It is worth considering why. It is, in any case, a journey and a lesson that finds little place in Freud's account of religion.

Psychoanalytic studies generally focus on the experience of the believer – or, as Jones (1991, 113) wrote:

... my purpose, however, is not to prove the existence of a divine being but only to discuss the psychological dynamics of religious experiences.... For my purposes, starting with the sacred means starting with the *human experience* of the sacred. (author's emphasis)

Today, most psychoanalytic studies focus on the transferential quality of the experience of the sacred: the way in which a person brings to bear (i.e., projects) his or her feelings about relationships with parents and others to his or her image of God. As Jones said, "[t]here ought to be parallels between the transferential patterns in religion and other relations in a person's life" (Jones 1991, 68).

Theological approaches are different primarily in their search for a proper language to speak about God and a proper language and attitude by which to interpret His presence in the world. God remains outside, as He surely must, but the task of humans is to develop a way of speaking and acting toward Him and toward each other in light of our knowledge of God. Langdon Gilkey (2001, 26) summarized the "theology of society" of Reinhold Niebuhr this way:

The task of theology is no longer merely the elucidation of doctrines from the sources of scripture and tradition, nor merely the effort to prove by reason

---

[1] In the Hebrew Bible, Sheol, the abode of the dead, is portrayed as a place where both the bad and the good, the pious and the wicked, reside after death, asleep in the dust in everlasting silence and oblivion. Sheol is perhaps best compared to Hades in fifth-century Greek myth.

the validity of Christian affirmations. It is now even more the interpretation of the mystery and travail of human existence, social history, and personal history by means of the symbols of Christian faith, to show that it is these symbols, and these alone, that make sense of the confusions of ordinary life.

About the Book of Job, the liberation theologian, Gustavo Gutiérrez (2003, xviii), stated the problem simply and starkly:

> The point of view that I myself adopt in this book is important and classic, and I believe, central to the book itself: the question of *how we are to talk about God*. More particularly, how we are to talk about God from within a specific situation – namely, the suffering of the innocent. (author's emphasis)

I approach the Book of Job from the perspective of transitional space, a concept developed by the English psychoanalyst D. W. Winnicott. The approach here considers both God and Job as leading characters in the text that is the Book of Job. Another advantage of turning to Winnicott is that his concept of *holding* – the practice that creates transitional space – helps to explain the type of understanding Primo Levi so longed to find but which seemed to forever escape him, particularly toward the end of his life. Nevertheless, the focus in this chapter is on Job, not Levi – although I draw on a story, "Titanium," from Levi's *Periodic Table* (1984) to illustrate the concept of holding.

Later in the chapter, I draw on another aspect of Winnicott's work, what he calls the "ruthless use of the object." There, the focus changes from Job to God, asking why God would treat Job with such pitiless abandon. Once again, I must caution the reader who may be appalled that anyone would be so presumptuous as to psychoanalyze God. Not God but rather the characters called God and Job in the Book of Job are my subjects.

God of Abjection, God of Holding

God does not frequently appear in the Old Testament, but neither is His appearance, what is called *theophany*, vanishingly rare. He speaks to Moses from a burning bush and from Mount Sinai (Exodus, 3:1–6; 19:3–25; 24:9–11). God speaks to Elijah (or perhaps one should simply say that God is present to Elijah) in the silence that follows the wind, the earthquake, and the fire (1 Kings, 19:11–13). The Lord makes several other appearances, but in none does He reveal His character as He does in His speeches from the whirlwind in the Book of Job (38–41). Because I am interested in God's character as it is revealed to us in those texts called Holy Scripture, the Book of Job is especially relevant.

A remarkable aspect of God's speeches from the whirlwind is that after His initial burst of sarcastic anger, Job serves as little more than an audience for God's soliloquy on the wonders of His creation. To be sure, God begins in anger, which takes the famous form of asking Job, "Where were you when I laid the foundations of the earth? Speak if you have understanding" (38:4). "Where were you when I separated the earth from the seas? When did you ever give the dawn its orders, assign the rising sun its post?" (38:12). Soon, however, God seems to tire of baiting Job, even as the poem continues to utilize the form of rhetorical query. Instead, God becomes transfixed by the beauty and the wonder of His creation. Indeed, one has the impression that it was no easy task.

> To walk the depths of the sea
> To see behind the gates of death. [The poet does not assume, it seems, that God created these gates too.]
> To conduct the light from its home, and back again.
> To loose the lightning, and have it say, as it travels to earth, "Your servant!"
> Do you bring out the stars as they are due?
> Guide the Great Bear and her young?
> Do you know the laws that rule the sky?
> And can you make it control the earth? (38:16–33, omitting lines)

On and on God goes, His questions becoming more elaborate, so that they soon become short essays on the beauty and wonder of the universe that He has created. What is the tone of these essays? One would have to say that God is enchanted with His creation, that He shares something with the stallion He created.

> Do you give the stallion his strength?
> Do you clothe his neck in a fearsome mane?
> Do you make him thunder like a locust swarm?
> .... Thrilled with his own force. (39:19–25, omitting lines)

Through it all, God mentions barely a word about humans or their place in His creation. God's second reply to Job, which many scholars see as yet another addition by a later redactor – so different is its tone, with its shift from an extreme naturalism to myth – contains a passing reference to His ability to subdue the proud and the cruel (40:11–13). However, this reference does not even begin to rise to the level of Deuteronomic theology. The context is whether Job has the power to do what God can do.

The content of God's second speech from the whirlwind is once again nature poetry, although of a much more obscure and mysterious kind in which God idealizes the power of two dragon-like monsters that he has created, generally called Behemoth (40: 15–24) and Leviathan (41). Liminal, resembling the hippopotamus and crocodile but much larger and more terrifying, especially the second, both are creatures of land and water. The first is passive in its power, able the swallow whole rivers. The second resembles a malicious dragon that breathes fire.[2] The point seems to be that only God could create such fearsome creatures and only God could master them.

What are we to think about this God? That He has no pity or moral consolation to offer humanity? That He is not a God who cares for humans? Indeed, He is not a God who seems to pay much attention to humans. God's initial encounter with Satan was evidently a rare distraction. God is primarily interested in pondering the perfection of His creation. The true or inner righteousness of characters like Job seems but a passing interest of God when compared to His true concern: contemplating the sublime wonder of His kingdom.

To be sure, there is consolation for humans in knowing this. Some One is in charge. The world is planned, plenitudinous, and beautiful – as sublime as God imagines. God has created a masterpiece that takes humans out of their little life and causes us to experience awe. The God of Job is not a jealous God. He is quite literally a careless God, possibly a lonely God, who needs to share His creation and the hard work behind it, but He is not a God who cares for humans.

Fortunately, humans are aesthetic creatures, able to find satisfaction and comfort in the beauty and sublimity of God's creation; however, in

---

[2] Bloom (2005, 226–7) suggested that Leviathan foretells the tyranny of nature and, ultimately, death over man. Bloom's reading is suggestive but fails to account for the limited role of this image in the Book of Job (as well as its likely late editorial insertion), which does, indeed, concern humanity's relationship to nature: gift and curse of a departed God.

what this satisfaction consists we need to be clear. It does not consist in what Gutiérrez says it consists. "Job is invited to sing with Yahweh the wonders of creation – without forgetting the source of it all is the free and gratuitous love of God" (1987, 75). One has to look very hard, from somewhere deep in the pages of the New Testament, to find an invitation from God to Job to join Him in a duet.

Here is how God – truly a God of nature when he speaks from the whirlwind – speaks to the condition of the absurd, as Camus (1955, 28) defines it: man cries out to the world that it acknowledge his existence, and the world is silent. After reading Job, we may say that once the Creator of nature spoke, and that although He did not invite man to join Him in singing nature's praises, God pointed out the marvels of His handiwork so that we might be ever more deeply spellbound by its sublimity. In this experience, absurdity melts away for a little while. One might feel small or insignificant in comparison to God's creation, but that is not the same as absurd, for one still partakes, if only for a moment, in the greatest show on earth: the universe.

What about feeling abject? Yes, the sublime is the abject in the dimension of beauty and wonder and terror and awe. If one thinks of the abject as the threatened dissolution of boundaries, then this is, of course, precisely the appeal of the sublime, precisely how Kant defines the term, that experience of excess that threatens to make mincemeat of human categories. According to Kristeva (1982, 207), the sublime and the transcendent – that is, art and religion – both deal with that archaic space where the familiar binaries such as self/other, or subject/object, have broken down or threaten to break down.

It is thus not lack of cleanliness or health that causes abjection, but what disturbs identity, system, order.... The in-between, the ambiguous, the composite. The traitor, the liar, the criminal with a good conscience. (1982, 4)

Abjection has the quality of the scapegoat, the *pharmakos* (the Greek term for scapegoat that also means both poison and cure), the traitor, the slimy viscous boundary violator, that which does not stay in its place. Oedipus is exemplary (Kristeva 1982, 85).

The In-Between Is Also Transitional Space

Take this same in-between space, both inside and outside, me and not me, and look at it from another perspective; it becomes what

Winnicott (1989) called *transitional space*: a space in which not abjection but rather quite the opposite feeling – the feeling of being held
and contained – is the leading affect. Transitional space represents a
dimension of experience that belongs neither to internal nor external
reality. Rather, it is that place where creative illusion meets objective
reality, the former creating the latter, but not really. Reality was already
there; however, for reality to truly feel separate and real, we must experience the illusion of having created it.

...the exciting thing about the curtain in a theater. When it goes up, each
one of us will create the play that is going to be enacted, and afterwards we
may even find that the overlap of what we have created...provides material
for a discussion about the play that was enacted. (1986, 133)

   Transitional space is first experienced when a child is held by its
mother or another caretaker. If mother is in tune with her child, which
means that she neither crushes the child with her anxiety nor drops
the child with her distraction and mental absence, the child does
not have to even think, "I feel held." Instead, the child is free to be.
Holding begins with the way in which the mother and others handle
the baby, but it comes to include all of the ways in which civilization
acts to help us find a place in this world. Or, as Winnicott said, "I
have used the term *cultural experience* as an extension of the idea of
transitional phenomena and of play" (1971, 99).
   What makes the difference as to whether this in-between space is
experienced as abjection or as being held? Although the answer is
surely complex, it depends in good measure on whether one sees
the world through the eyes of Kristeva or Winnicott. I am not being
flippant. Abjection *is* the foil of being held. Abjection is the:

...immemorial violence with which a body becomes separated from another
body in order to be – maintaining that night in which the outline of the
signified thing vanishes and where only the imponderable affect is carried
out. (Kristeva 1982, 10)

Holding, on the other hand, maintains the outline of signified. One is
held by the outline of the vanished object. To be held in this way is to
be rendered real, to exist in the imaginary real of transitional space.[3]

---

3 Unlike Jacques Lacan, who also wrote about the real, Kristeva did not hold that "the
   real is the impossible" (Lacan 1977, x). For Lacan, the *real* is a hole, a void, a term used

It is time to return to a question deferred previously: How close can we come to Job's experience as we read the Book of Job? Fairly close, suggested Kristeva (1982, 29), for all artistic experience, including religion, is "an impure process that protects from the abject only by dint of being immersed in it."

To make sense of Kristeva's statement (i.e., to render it less abstract so that it might be criticized), I turn to Scheindlin (1998, 26), whose prose translation of the Book of Job seeks to preserve the original poetic rhythm of the Hebrew verse, which employed a considerably looser meter than traditional English verse. For Scheindlin, "Job has grasped and intrepidly maintained the most terrifying reality" (1998, 17), which is that Job is just and God is not. Every heresy that Job commits was, in fact, the brutal truth. The Book of Job is consolation not in its theological content but rather as a work of poetry – that is, as a work created by and for other humans. Poetry frames and forms our anger, our grief, our rage – giving us a chance to share in Job's experience of these emotions and so come to find a place for them in our own life (Scheindlin 1998, 22–5).

Scheindlin approaches the Book of Job much as Aristotle approached Greek tragedy, defining *tragedy* as the *katharsis* of pity and fear (*Poetics*, c. 6). Although Scheindlin does not elaborate on katharsis, we must to understand the full import of his argument. By katharsis, Aristotle did not mean purgation but rather the clarification of these emotions so that the soul, or psyche, might find a proper place for them. Drawing on her rich discussion of the etymological origins of the term *katharsis* in words used to refer to clarity and lack of obstruction, Martha Nussbaum argued that the term is best translated as "clarification." The function of tragedy is to accomplish through pity and fear a "clarification (or illumination) concerning experiences of the pitiable and fearful kind" (Nussbaum 1986, 389–98). In doing this, we find a proper place for these emotions in our psyches. *Katharsis* is the clarification and acceptance of the most difficult emotions; it never meant a mere purging of emotion.

to describe all that is lacking, and must be lacking, in the symbolic order. We know the real only by its absence, what cannot be expressed. For Kristeva, conversely, the real is experienced in events such as melancholy and catastrophic suffering, inscribing itself in the rhythms of the body in such a way that it can eventually be accessed by the speaking subject, whom she understood to be a living, breathing loving body (Kristeva 1996, 22–3).

The horror and the pity, rendered in rhythmic form (Greek tragedy was spoken in rhyme, while the chorus sang its lines) and so expressed in a form that does not fragment our souls, allows us to know the terrible truth that Job knew. This *is* the katharsis: terrible truths made knowable – in this case, via their expression in rhythmic form. Nietzsche was getting at a related point in *The Birth of Tragedy out of the Spirit of Music*, although it is worth distinguishing between the disease of everyday life (which Nietzsche evidently experienced so keenly) and the afflictions of Job:

Conscious of the truth he has once seen, man now sees everywhere only the horror or absurdity of existence... he is nauseated. Here, when the danger to his will is greatest, *art* approaches as a saving sorceress, expert at healing. She alone knows how to turn these nauseous thoughts about the horror or absurdity of existence into notions with which one can live: these are the *sublime* as the artistic taming of the horrible, and the *comic* as the artistic discharge of the nausea of absurdity. (Nietzsche 1968b, 60; emphasis his)

Poetry is the rhythmic lullaby, the rocking of the cradle, the comfort of the song that frames and forms the terrible truth. Only in that particularly human form – the rhythmic form, the forms of song, dance, music, and poetry, all of which mimic our earliest sensations of being held and soothed – can we bear to know the terrible truth. In fact, this is almost exactly how Kristeva came to define the *chora*. It is a

... *rhythmic space*, which has no thesis, and no position, the process by which significance is constituted. Plato himself leads us to such a process when he calls this receptacle or *chora* nourishing and maternal. (Kristeva 1984, 26; my emphasis)

By "no thesis, and no position," Kristeva seemed to mean what Winnicott meant: that the rhythmic holding environment responds to the rhythm of another, often in a different register. Mother coos when baby smiles or I feel sad when you have suffered a disappointment and you can see it in the slump of my shoulders. In *attunement*, as it is called, your feelings evoke comparable but not identical reactions in me. Attunement is emotional rhythm. It is through this rhythm that the holding environment fades into the background, becomes the background. A perfect holding environment would be imperceptible. In a perfect holding environment, baby would never grow up. Needed is not perfect parenting but rather the "good-enough mother," as Winnicott (1971, 10) called her.[4]

Winnicott referred to experiences of separation, experiences that indeed may be experienced as a type of "immemorial violence," in terms of the "I AM" moment, a raw moment in which:

The new individual feels infinitely exposed. Only if someone has her arms around the infant at this time can the I AM moment be endured, or rather, perhaps, risked. (Winnicott 1965a, 148)

Scheindlin's point, with which Winnicott (1986, 36) would surely have agreed, is that for adults, cultural forms such as poetry can take on this holding function, containing the individual so that he or she does not feel infinitely exposed when confronted with a world not made for the human being. For this is precisely the world that God reveals to Job – the same world the Book of Job reveals to us but in such a beautiful poetic form that we are able to stand it.

Job's experience is not quite the same. Not the rhythm of the experience but rather something about the fact that the world that does not care is revealed to him by a God who does not care allows Job to mourn what it means to be human. Winnicott said that the only way to appreciate transitional space is not to push the paradox, not to ask whether it is really me or not me. Perhaps it is time to appreciate Job's ability to grasp God's irony: the God who does not care introduces Job to a nature that does not care but, somehow in the end, Job feels cared for by God – or rather held by God's world: they amount to almost the same thing.

The result is that whereas Job is abject, he does not experience God's world as absurd, even as neither God nor His world ever answer him in human terms. (Absurdity, operating in the realm of the symbolic, is particularly destructive of meaning when it prevents abjection from being symbolically framed and formed – what Kristeva called *purification*, which is discussed in more detail in Chapter 4.) If Job experienced the world as absurd, then presumably he could not mourn.

---

4 Kristeva went beyond Winnicott, idealizing the cocooned state of the *chora*, as though the very young child never experiences discomfort and need. "According to Kristeva, our first experience is of a realm of plenitude, of a oneness with our environment, and with the semiotic *chora*" (McAfee 2004, 45). One can glimpse Rousseau lurking in the background.

The inability to mourn stems from, above all, the inability to stop holding oneself – that is, from the inability to stop holding all the bits and pieces of oneself together out of fear that if one doesn't, then one will fall apart, go insane. The task of the therapist, said Winnicott, is not always to interpret; the therapeutic task is to create a supportive environment, thereby allowing the patient to mourn. "This 'holding,' like the task of the mother in infant-care, acknowledges tacitly the tendency of the patient to disintegrate, to cease to exist, to fall forever" (Winnicott 1965b, 241).

God has revealed to Job that he lives in a world that is sufficiently ordered and purposeful that even if Job is incapable of understanding this order, he can let himself go and just be. Be what? Be abject, certainly, but not merely abject. Job can be the human abject, human enough to mourn the fact that he – like us – remains a dying animal.

Neither Job nor the readers of the Book of Job – at least, as the experience of reading the Book of Job is accounted for by Kristeva (1982) and Scheindlin (1998) – are enabled by God to appreciate the particulars of His handiwork. Creation by creation, creature by creature, constellation by constellation (or so it seems), God lays out His Kingdom, as though He would have us appreciate every sparrow, every horse, every vulture, every season, every snowflake, every life, every death. However, the sublime overwhelms not just human categories but also the human capacity to appreciate details and distinctions. The sublime shatters categories and in this way prepares us for new experiences. However, the way in which God presents the sublime – that is, as an inventory of His creations (admittedly only a partial catalogue) – does little to allow us to appreciate the unique particularity of God's creations.

This is so for two reasons. First, God presents most of his creations as unique genera: the horse, the vulture, the sparrow, the stars. We are called on to appreciate every snowflake, not because each snowflake is different from all the rest but rather because the Lord God made them all.[5] Second, appreciating the unique particularity of the other requires that one feel securely held. In states of anxiety, including states of extreme suffering, subtle distinctions are the first to disappear

---

[5] God talks about His creation of snow and hail (38:22) but not about snowflakes; that further distinction is my example.

because the world is divided into dualistic categories such as purity and danger, pain and relief from pain, victim and executioner, the edible and the inedible, a safe place to hide and an unsafe place to hide.

The security of being held is never achieved in Kristeva's account. For Kristeva, the sublime remains forever bound to its dark twin: abjection. Although Scheindlin's agenda has little to do with appreciating the particular and nothing to do with using the particular as a back door to the sublime, his account of the soothing, rhythmic quality of the poetic form allows for the possibility that one might experience the sublime while feeling securely held. If so, then the possibility exists that the sublime might not swamp particularity but rather open us to it. I return to a version of this question in Chapter 5, asking what transcendence might look like in a world in which not the sublime but rather the absurd is the leading experience of the age.

In "Titanium," one of the elements of *The Periodic Table*, Levi tells the story of a little girl alone with a great big strange man, who is painting her family's apartment white. First, she wonders how all that white could be "contained in so small a can." Then, she asks why it is so white. The painter replies, "Titanium, the pigment."

However, she hears the Italian words, *Ti taglio*, which mean, "I cut you." "Maria felt a delicious shiver of fear run through her" (Levi 1984, 166). She is more excited than frightened; so excited that she approaches the man from behind, as though she will get as close as she can to the wet paint. Suddenly, he turns, takes a piece of chalk out his pocket, draws a circle on the floor around Maria, and says, "You must stay in there."

Maria sat on her heels and considered the circle for a long time . . . but she became convinced that there was no way out. She tried to rub at one spot with her finger and saw that the chalk line actually disappeared; but she understood very well that the man would not have regarded that system as valid. The circle was evidently magical. (Levi 1984, 167)

Eventually, the man leaves. As he is packing up his things, taking them to his truck, Maria called out – but not too loudly, for she was afraid he might hear. Finally, the man returned to the kitchen and Maria asks if she can come out. "Of course you may," the man replies. Picking up a rag, he "wiped away the circle very carefully to undo the enchantment. When the circle had disappeared, Maria got up and left, skipping, and she felt very happy and satisfied" (Levi 1984, 168).

This is how holding works. Maria, we may surmise, was frightened not just by the big strange man but also by her own desires – perhaps for the man in ways she didn't yet understand. One could play psychological games with "I cut you" and losing her virginity, but Levi provides no warrant for that. It seems more likely that Maria was frightened by her desire for something more abstract, such as the desire to spoil his work or even perhaps to lose herself in all that white. Levi suggested no answers to these questions, but we do have the sense that Maria was at risk of losing control and needed to be held – not to be physically contained or restrained by the strange man: that would have been unnecessary and too frightening. Instead, the man came up with the perfect game, an enchanted chalk circle. (I use the term *game* not to render it less serious, only to suggest that both sides must play by the rules to make it real.) There, Maria is held because she wants to be – held, not crushed – held but not held hostage or prisoner; just held until the man releases her at just the right moment and she can skip away.

Levi, it turns out, was fascinated by containers. In "A Bottle of Sunshine" (1989), written in 1985, he proposed in a humorous but revealing vein a new definition of man: not *homo sapiens*, or *homo faber*, or *homo ludens* but rather the animal who makes containers.[6] He included a long and imaginative list of containers, some of which are not obviously containers (e.g., frosted glass) that admit light but not images. Others are containers, such as cupped hands. Never, however, did he refer to the entire human body as a container (Angier 2002, 682–4). Our future, Levi concluded, depends entirely on whether scientists can find containers for some of our most fearsome energies, including hydrogen, which powers the sun and the atomic bomb.

In her biography, Carole Angier made much of Levi's need to be contained or held. Being held or contained:

. . . touches on themes – even obsessions – which profoundly move him. . . . Containing . . . imprisoning – these are ideas which push him into imagery,

---

[6] If one were going to take Levi's definition seriously, he would, of course, be mistaken. Birds make nests, bees make honeycombs, and foxes and wolves have their dens. There is nothing unique about man as the container-making animal.

because they attract and repel him equally.... Which does he want or fear more, to escape or remain contained? I think he could never say. (2002, 683)

Angier built her biography around this theme, arguing that in choosing his wife, Lucia, Levi chose a woman whom he hoped would contain or hold him – and ended up with a woman who took him prisoner, just as his mother did (2002, 728, passim).

One could put the same facts together another way, keeping in mind that the artist is just like the rest of us, only more so – to paraphrase Freud about neurotics. In other words, Levi was extraordinarily sensitive to the problem of holding, of how easy it is to move from feeling held to feeling crushed or dropped. Surely, Levi had experiences of both. Furthermore, some experiences, such as the Lager (concentration camp), are both at once. The Lager is a hydraulic press designed to squeeze the last drop of humanity and life out of the container that is the human body before disposing of the empty husk. At the same time, the Lager is a terrifying void, in which all stability and order and meaning and purpose and predictability have vanished, leaving the prisoner to fall forever. (In the next chapter, we hear testimony from a survivor who suffered for years from terrifying dreams of being offered up to a giant hydraulic press.) It is small wonder that such a sensitive man as Levi was particularly aware of the precious and precarious boundaries that separate each of us from being crushed or dropped. Perhaps this made Levi more vulnerable in some ways, but one wants to be careful about turning insight into illness.

God's Ruthless Use of Job

The Book of Job was not the first work of Western literature to address the suffering of the righteous. Unique to the Book of Job is the opening frame scene, the way it lets us in on the negotiations between God and Satan. What we learn depends on where we start. The pious reader (including the reader who can imagine what it would be like to be pious) learns to read the Book of Job as a theologically astute attempt to distinguish conventional from internal or actual piety. Job was hubristic and arrogant; he thought he deserved the good things God had bestowed on him. The Book of Job is a journey through affliction, by which Job learns his proper place in the universe.

The less pious and more literal reader learns another lesson: that God torments Job to win a bet with Satan, to prove to Satan the righteousness of His servant Job. If God were not God, we would call Him selfish, egocentric, and narcissistic: a user of others as a means to His own glorification.

However, God is God, so those categories do not apply. Still, the reader may wonder whether approaching the Book of Job from a psychological perspective is compatible with viewing the Book of Job as a sacred text. To be sure, a psychoanalytic interpretation is incompatible with any interpretation that regards the Book of Job as the literal word of God. Because that concept makes no sense to begin with, we can dismiss it out of hand. How could a work of poetry (all but three of the forty-two chapters are in verse) employing symbol, metaphor, and imagery be literal? For in the sense that "a literal reading of the Bible" is generally used, the phrase means a reading that abjures allegory, metaphor, or allusion – the literary devices from which almost any work of poetry, including the Book of Job, is constructed. If, however, by the term *sacred text* one means to say that the story it conveys is the inspired word of God, there is no reason that my account is incompatible with a view that regards the Bible as sacred text. To be sure, my view is heresy to some, but that is a different matter; heresy is only possible among the believers.

It is not uncommon today to think about God, particularly the Old Testament God, as participating in a process of learning and development. A God who learns is the explicit teaching of "open theism," as it is called (Hasker 1998). A God whose development includes learning is implicit in process theology (Cobb and Griffin 1976), an outgrowth of the process philosophy of Alfred North Whitehead.[7] However, we need not turn to tributary theologies to make this point; simply read the Old Testament, as Christians call it. There, God frequently seems

---

[7] The reasonings of open theism (Hasker 1998) and process philosophy are different. Whereas both hold that God's knowledge of the future is imperfect because the nature of the future is to consist of possibilities, not certainties, only process philosophy, as developed by Whitehead (1978), holds that God's power over each individual is limited because each individual has its own power. The more complex the individual, the more powerful the individual, and humans are the most complex individuals of all.

to change His mind and, in the process, learns something about Himself and the world.

In Exodus 32:14, in answer to Moses' prayer, "the Lord repented of the evil which He thought to do unto his people." In fact, the Lord repents (*nacham*) of His destructive thoughts and acts toward His chosen people and others many times. After the fall of Judah, Jeremiah receives word from God to those who remain: "I repent of the evil that I have done to you" (26:19). In most cases, when God changes His mind, He is regretting or repenting that He has acted destructively in haste and anger, as in Judges 2:18; II Samuel 24:16; Psalm 106:45; Psalm 135:14; and Jeremiah 26:19.[8] Indeed, in Exodus 33:3, God tells Moses that He will not go with him into the land of milk and honey because He might become so angry at this stiff-necked people – so keen to worship idols – that He would once again be overcome with rage and destroy them.

To be sure, some of the preceding cases of God's "repentance" require qualification. At times, God "repents" because the people in question – generally, but not always, Israelites – repent and change their ways first. God's "repentance" is sometimes the result of His prophets' warnings having the desired effect. Nevertheless, it seems fair to say that the God of the Old Testament is emotionally labile, quick to anger, and God enough to repent of His anger.

This is not quite what happens in the Book of Job. Here, I am going to read the story neither as a pious nor impious reader (the two possibilities mentioned previously) but rather from a third position, one that imagines what God Himself might have to learn from tormenting Job. We have seen what Job learns from his affliction. Does God learn anything from afflicting Job? Or is that itself an impious question? In any case, it is the question I am asking, drawing on what Winnicott called the "ruthless use of the object" to do so.

---

[8] The Hebrew for *repent* is *nacham*. It also means "relented" and suggests that one is relieved at not having taken a planned but now recognized as undesirable course of action. Different translations of the Bible render the term differently. Of Jeremiah 26:19, the New American Standard Bible (NASB) says "changed His mind." The New International Version (NIV) and New King James Version (NKJV) say "relent," whereas the King James Version (KJV), the Revised Standard Version (RSV), and the 1901 American Standard Version (ASV) say "repent." www.carm.org/open/Jer26_19.htm.

Today, Winnicott's view of transitional experience constitutes the leading psychoanalytic framework within which religion is understood (Jones, 1991; Ulanov 2001). One reason is because Winnicott was sympathetic to religion:

> To the child who develops "belief in" can be handed the god of the house-hold or of the society. . . . But to the child with no "belief in" god is at best a pedagogue's gimmick, and at worst . . . evidence . . . that the parent-figures are lacking in confidence in the processes of human nature and are frightened of the unknown. (Winnicott 1965b, 93)

The other reason Winnicott's psychoanalytic theory is useful for think-ing about religion is that his account of how we create what is already there lends itself to a nondogmatic belief in God. More precisely, it lends itself to a way of thinking about God in which the question "But does God *really* exist?" is not so central, not so important.

Helpful as this aspect of Winnicott's work is in thinking about God, it is not the part on which I am going to draw, at least not directly. Instead, I want to use Winnicott to address the question of why God torments Job so. Why does God treat Job with such utter ruthlessness? My answer, following Winnicott, is that because in transitional space, the space in which God creates Job (and not just vice versa), the ruthless, destructive use of the object – in this case, Job – is the way we come to understand and appreciate the separate existence of the object. Still new to the act of creation, God had yet to learn this about one of His creations: humanity.

To be sure, Job acts with a certain manic ruthlessness, not merely in his desire to put God behind bars, so to speak, but also in the way he would treat God as a virtual equal in debate, if only he could. Job would belittle God, turning Him into a human on a larger scale. The very assumption is so arrogant that it seems only right to call it ruthless. Here, I am less interested in Job's psychology than God's. If it is itself arrogant to psychoanalyze God, let the reader remember that I am actually analyzing a character in a text who is called Yahweh (but not by Job, who is a gentile) to uncover the insight of those who wrote the Book or to enhance the insight of those who read it – or both, depending on one's theory of reading.

Although he is best known for his account of transitional spaces and relationships, toward the end of his career, Winnicott turned to another way of thinking about relationships, what he came to call "the use of an object." The use of an object is marked by the ruthless exploitation of the other, the greedy consumption of everything the other has to offer and more.[9] That sounds bad. Winnicott thought it is good, for it is through this process that the reality of the external world is created: "It is the destructive drive that creates the quality of externality. This is central in the structure of my argument" (1989, 226) (if, that is, the object resists destruction). The result is not just the recognition of an objective reality outside the self but also frequently joy at a world outside me, one in which I might take pleasure. Only through the unsuccessful attempt to destroy objective reality do we come to recognize a reality separate and distinct from the self. Winnicott treated the ruthless use of an object as a type of communication, frequently inventing little dialogues (mock Punch-and-Judy dialogues, Adam Phillips [1988] called them) to illustrate the relationship:

The subject says to the object: 'I destroyed you,' and the object is there to receive the communication. From now on the subject says: 'Hullo object!' 'I destroyed you.' 'I love you. You have value for me because of your survival of my destruction of you. While I am loving you I am all the time destroying you in (unconscious) fantasy.' (Phillips 1988, 222)

Consider, Winnicott continued, a man who buys a beautiful painting. He cares for and protects the painting in order to destroy it in unconscious fantasy over and over again. If he didn't, he couldn't really relate to the painting; it would never be an independent source of enjoyment, one that "can feed back other-than-me substance" (Winnicott 1989, 227). Of course, if his painting were destroyed by a vandal, that would be entirely different; it would be the difference between fantasy and reality. It would not be, however, a difference in the strength of the destructive impulses, only in the ability to sublimate them creatively (1989, 232). Maturity is about destroying the object in fantasy so that one can use it in reality. "The price that has to be paid [for the reality of the external world] is acceptance of the ongoing destruction in unconscious fantasy" (1989, 223).

9 Seven papers "On 'The Use of an Object'" are collected in Winnicott (1989, 217–46). Rather than cite each paper separately, I cite the page numbers to this source.

Winnicott's idea is stranger than first appears. For Freud, one would destroy the object because it is beyond one's omnipotent control, because its independent reality frustrates the will. Winnicott said the opposite: it is the destructive impulse that creates the quality of externality, and it is this externality that makes the object available for satisfaction. With the term *creates*, Winnicott meant something like Kant's *synthetic a priori*: destructiveness allows us to discover in nature what our minds allow to be there, the real separateness of the object.

Not the act of reparation, by which we attempt to make amends for our destructiveness (Klein 1975) but rather the mother's continued survival in the face of her child's attacks is what makes not just a separate reality but also a valued one. The object survives on its own and the child is overjoyed. Now, the child has someone to use, which brings pleasure to both mother and child. People want to be used; it is a deep source of satisfaction. "For most people, the ultimate compliment is to be found and used" (Winnicott 1987, 103). Using and being used by other people is one of the ways people get close to one another, almost as though one could reach out and take what one needs from inside the other person. It sounds destructive, invasive – and it is – but only if we can't distinguish between reality and fantasy must it hurt the other.

If it is only through a ruthless encounter with the other that we become convinced of the other's separateness, then the absence of this encounter must make it seem as if the other is not only incredibly vulnerable (because one has not had the experience of the other successfully resisting one's attempts to destroy it) but also not quite separate. The other's otherness will continue to be recognized, but somewhere there will always be a doubt: if not about the other's otherness, then about the other's ability to survive – that is, to be autonomous and free.

Who Is This Creature Called Man or Woman?

What does all this have to do with God and Job? In tormenting Job, God is testing Job: not his piety, not his inward goodness (as distinct from his external displays of piety); God ruthlessly torments Job to determine what God has made. Think about it. God has only recently created the universe, still wet and shimmering. Does God really know who this creature called Job is? (Here, the generic quality of Job is relevant: neither Jew nor pagan nor Israelite, Job lives in the land of Uz, a strange land far from Israel; Job is everyman, the universal human.) God, we are told, made this man, every man and woman, in His own image (Genesis 1:27). But what does this mean?

Less and less, it seems, as we leave the moment of humanity's creation. Still, it remains an important question. Who is this creature God has created in His image? Is Job the man a failed creation? Can he survive on his own and maintain his moral compass? Will he survive God's withdrawal from this newly minted world? The last, it seems, is the key question. For it is in the Book of Job, as Jack Miles (1996, 404–6) pointed out in *God: A Biography*, that the God of the Old Testament withdraws from this world, never to reappear in such engaged form.

God's ruthlessness is not confined to his allowing Satan to physically torment Job. God is equally ruthless in failing to comfort Job once He makes His appearance in the whirlwind, an image of barely contained chaos – not comfort but rather, "Look around, what do you count in the scheme of things, what did you imagine you were doing trying to call me to account?" This is, in effect, what God says from the whirlwind. Neither is God necessarily being unkind, just ruthless – that is, without ruth, lacking in compassion or pity. Why? Because it appears as if God is about to take His leave from His creation. How far He plans to go and for how long remain uncertain. It still is. However, in the very act of showing Job all that He has created, coupled with His ruthless lack of compassion for Job, God seems to be asking, "Can you, creature called Job, steadfast everyman, survive as a decent human being once I take my leave? Are you separate enough? Strong enough? Good enough?"[10] Although the world of God and Job is patriarchal in the extreme, these questions are not unfamiliar to most parents who have sent a child off into the world.

Am I speculating? Of course, although nowhere in the Old Testament does God appear again as a character, even as He makes brief appearances, often to repent (Jeremiah 26:19). Only in the New Testament does God reappear as a character, in the very different

---

[10] Recall God's challenge at the very beginning of his lecture to Job, "Brace yourself like a man. I will question you, and you will answer me" (40:7). God is going to find out "what this man is made of," as we say today.

form of Jesus Christ. Is it any wonder, by the way, that Job – the most innocent and just of men who suffers for his goodness – is seen by many Christians as the prefiguration of Christ?

Chesterton (1916) wrote a short essay on the Book of Job, concluding that the Book is built on a paradox:

> In the prologue we see Job tormented not because he was the worst of men, but because he was the best. It is the lesson of the whole work that man is most comforted by paradoxes. Here is the very darkest and strangest of the paradoxes; and it is by all human testimony the most reassuring. I need not suggest what high and strange history awaited this paradox of the best man in the worst fortune. I need not say that in the freest and most philosophical sense there is one Old Testament figure who is truly a type; or say what is prefigured in the wounds of Job.

For Chesterton, Job is the only developed character – what he calls a "type" – other than God in the Old Testament.

Whereas such a reading has a virtue of making God a character, it is unhistorical, which has the effect of making God a less interesting character. Read in its Old Testament context, the Book of Job concerns God's struggle to separate from Job so that He might stand back from His creation. Fascinating is how God does so: by trying to destroy Job. Job's survival, his moral endurance – in which Job retains both his integrity as well as his ability to learn something radically new about God and himself (Job is both steadfast and able to transform himself – that is, able to learn) – allows God to step back from His creation, with all the consequences for good and evil that this entails. It is unfortunate that Job's combination of virtues – moral surety, coupled with an ability to remake himself in order to remain devout under radically changed circumstances – remains so rare.

Of course, God could simply crush Job like a bug, but God is not the art vandal about whom Winnicott wrote. God is the artist, the creator, who needs to be assured that His creation is good and separate enough to survive without Him. He does this first by tormenting that part of His creation that can talk back, and when it does, then telling it – that is, Job – that he had better learn to take life like a mature adult, that he is not so special, that he is only a small part of creation, and that he had best learn his place.

One imagines that theological assumptions might have psychoanalytic implications. Less obvious is how a psychoanalytic interpretation of God's relationship to Job has theological implications. It does. Most theologies hold that God created the world *ex nihilo*, out of nothing. This is how the first chapter and verse of Genesis is usually interpreted: "In the beginning, God created the heavens and the earth." However, those who see God as learning and developing over time reject *creatio ex nihilo* or give it a quite different meaning, suggesting that to create from nothing means to give form to chaos (Griffin 1981, 101–2). The account of creation in the Book of Job goes even further, suggesting not so much that God brought order out of chaos (*tohu wa-bohu*, a theme of significance to Primo Levi, discussed in Chapter 5), as that God struggled to bring order out of a multiplicity of forces, each a power in its own right (e.g., the sun, lightning, and thunder). In this regard, the model at work in Job comes closer to Plato's Demiurge in *The Timaeus* (30a–b), a craftsman who works with materials not readily malleable to his will. If this is so, then an account of God's ruthless use of Job – presumably, one of his more sophisticated and elaborate creations – to assure Himself of the separate reality and integrity of His creation makes even more sense. Human and divine creativity are not entirely different, even if they work on a vastly (by infinite orders of magnitude) different scale.

"You seem to have forgotten one thing," the thoughtful reader might reply. "You write as if you have forgotten that God of Job is, in fact, the literary creation of men. You write, in other words, as if you have forgotten the definition of belief, 'when the object created is in fact described as though it instead created you'" (Scarry 1985, 205). There would be some truth to such criticism, although it was Winnicott's great virtue to remind us that we do not always have to keep this definition in mind. Sometimes we can suspend disbelief, asking in all seriousness why God would be so terribly ruthless. Who knows, perhaps the suspension of disbelief will take us farther in the long run.

Just in case it doesn't, however, we can reframe the question. Not why is God so ruthless but rather why do humans so willingly – indeed, eagerly – attribute their suffering to God? For, as Elaine Scarry pointed out in "Body and Voice in the Judeo-Christian Scriptures," a chapter in *The Body in Pain*, throughout the Old Testament, God makes His invisible, disembodied presence known primarily through wounding human bodies. It is as though God and humanity are positioned vertically at the two opposite ends of a weapon: God at the handle, man at the tip. "At times, the image seems to define the structure of belief itself" (Scarry 1985, 183). In the Old Testament, God is the disembodied voice on the other side of a weapon. We, who suffer under the weapon, become His body, His reality, through our suffering (208).

Why? Because all too soon, humanity's power of creativity, the long lists of begetting, as in "Seth begat Enosh who begat Kenan who begat Enoch who begat Ham who begat...," begin to take on a strictly human power, the power of bodily generation. Wounding by God, on the other hand, continually "re-enacts the creation because it re-enacts the power of alteration that has its first profound occurrence in creation." Furthermore, only in wounding does the invisible God become visible, inscribed in the human body. "In... wounding, the graphic image of the human body substitutes for the object of belief that itself has no content and which cannot be represented" (Scarry 1985, 183, 198).[11]

Seen from this perspective, men would write about God's ruthless use of Job's body, men would willingly attribute their affliction to God, in order to make Him real, to continue the process of creation, to keep the process – that is, to keep God – alive and in their presence. Yet, notice here the almost inevitable tendency to confuse creation and destruction, as though torment and death were a sign of life. Primo Levi participates in this confusion and is discussed in Chapter 4.

Undoing Confusion

Scarry argued that this confusion begins to be undone in the Old Testament, as the Hebrews make objects that successfully embody God, without trying to re-create God's body as an idol such as the golden calf. Exemplary are sacred objects such as an ark, an altar, a written song, a robe, a recorded commandment. The human body need no

[11] Contrary to Kristeva, wounding and its correlates do not necessarily constitute an experience of abjection that must be purified. Much Biblical wounding, epitomized by Christ's crucifixion, is not a mark of abjection that must be purified. Wounding is a sign of the sacred that is already sanctified.

longer be the sole object on which God's body is inscribed. The sacred artifact can take the place of the body. In the New Testament, God receives a body, one that is itself the subject of affliction – the cross a weapon that is all tip and no handle, so to speak, the Lord impaled on it (Scarry 1985, 222–3).

For all her Biblical examples of affliction, Scarry (1985, 183) never referred to the Book of Job and only once possibly alluded to it in passing. To be sure, Job's affliction is redundant in the sense that it serves, like so much Biblical affliction, to give voice and presence to God's silence. However, the Book of Job is unusual – indeed, unique – in the degree to which it portrays God reflecting on His work of creation. To be sure, we are told about God's creation in Genesis (1– 2:25), but the details are limited. More limited still is God's pride, his "emotional investment," as we say today. In the Book of Job, however, God Himself is thrilled, evidently still awed, at His creation – above all, at the forces He had to overcome to make this beautiful world.

Here, I suggest, is how we may participate in God's world; indeed, we may read the Book of Job as an invitation to do so. What renders the world holy, sacred, and sublime is the way in which the diversity and wonder of worldly beauty overwhelms human categories, becoming "the beginning of terror we are still just able to bear" (Rilke 2000, *Duino Elegies*, first elegy). The experience is analogous to the Biblical experience of encountering God – especially God's face – an experience so shattering that hardly anyone survives (there are exceptions; see Exodus 33:11). The result is that the world itself becomes God-like, numinous, awesome. One might say that the world becomes what God's body would be if God had a body.

One might be inclined to see a certain primitivism in this way of thinking. If so, one should ask whether it is obvious that more abstract formulations of the Judeo-Christian tradition, in which (as they say) Augustine baptizes Plato and Aquinas grants communion to Aristotle, are truly more advanced. Taking the Book of Job seriously in its own right reveals the odd alliance of the particular and the sublime in God's world, our world. The sublime may shatter human categories but not because it is abstract – on the contrary, because the sublime is so concrete, so real. The sublime is Antoine Roquentin's chestnut tree, an image from Sartre's *Nausea*, experienced for just a moment in such a way that we no longer wish to replace it with our idea of the tree but rather to experience the tree as though it and we were the only realities on earth (Sartre 1964, 125–9). To know this is the beginning of worship. What a secular version of transcendence might look like, a transcendence that begins and ends with the particular, is explored in Chapter 5. I do not forget to ask whether an experience of transcendence devoted to the particular is really transcendence at all.

To Know the Truth and Live

Although one may read the Book of Job as an invitation from God to know and worship Him through His creation, this remains a perilous reading, one that risks succumbing to the same temptation as Gutiérrez: an over-eagerness to attribute goodness and love to God that is unwarranted by the text. Seen immanently (i.e., strictly from the text we call the Book of Job) and not from a perspective that looks back at Job from the revelation of Christ, it appears that God has gone from crushing Job to dropping Job. Recall that these are the two extremes of transitional space, the two ways in which transitional space may fail: mothers or others may be so demanding, intrusive, and invasive that they crush the life out of their children; conversely, mothers may be so distracted, obtuse, and absent that they abandon their children, providing no holding at all. Odd but true is the degree to which mothers and others may do both of these at once. Might one even say this about God, who sends Satan to torment Job, finally appearing before Job only to abandon him to the universe?

Yet, it cannot be that simple either, for in the end, Job is satisfied. God has spoken and Job feels redeemed, albeit in a way he evidently never imagined. For Job has come to understand not just God but also himself and his place in the universe in a new way. Indeed, this is the most striking thing we learn about Job: not just that he misunderstood God but also that he had misunderstood himself, for he had failed to understand himself in the order of things. God has shown him that, and Job is grateful, taking comfort in the signs of his mortality: dust and ashes (42:5–6). Job feels comforted and contained by this God, who seems to offer no comfort at all. For the reader who is not pious, which is not the same as impious, this comfort is primarily aesthetic. We are told a tale about God's caprice (albeit solely from the perspective of human happiness) in the rhythmic form of poetry, a form that is sufficiently soothing so that we can use it as a medium by which to learn or, rather, bear the truth.

A related reading assumes that the authors of the Book of Job were trying to convey a somewhat different message about God. If we take seriously Elihu's introduction of God's speeches from the whirlwind, in which he uses many of the same images of nature's power and beauty to represent God (32–37) that God Himself employs, then it may be incorrect to conclude that God has carelessly placed man into His wondrous creation. Rather, God Himself is being virtually equated with nature in order to capture God's absolute otherness. Nature is metaphor for God's otherness, not His carelessness.

What imagery better captures otherness, difference, and distance than the unpredictable and powerful aspects of nature, from lightning to thunderbolts to lions to eagles, especially to a people who live virtually their entire lives outdoors? Not once does God mention a domesticated creature, only wild ones.[12] It would be pantheism to say that God is represented as being in these phenomena or creatures, and He is not so represented. He is represented as their creator. However, Elihu's introduction of God as the hidden power behind nature's grandness (37:21–24), coupled with God's justification of His power (God is doing no less) in terms of His mastery of nature, could lead one to conclude that the authors intended the reader to identify God with nature's otherness and to stop thinking of God as a superhuman, as Job does when he wishes he could take God to court (9:32–35). When Job finally says to God, "I see how little I am. I will not answer you," it is as though he recognizes that one cannot put the universe on trial (40:4).

Job has moved from seeing power as persecution to power as an awesome mystery, before which he must make his peace. Job recants, but it appears from the context that he does not now hold himself guilty, as once he held himself righteous but persecuted. Rather, Job

---

[12] The horse to which God refers (39:19–25) is a partial exception to this claim. The horse is evidently bridled and ready for war (an anachronism given the likely dramatic date of circa 1000 BCE), but it acts under its own raw power and enthusiasm. Its rider is never mentioned. Earlier (39:9–11), God wonders if Job (and one should read "humanity" here) will be able to harness the unicorn and, more interesting still, will Job be able to trust this creature to do his will.

recognizes that categories of guilt and innocence, particularly as they are applied to oneself as an act of self-justification, are irrelevant. God knows, God will decide, and Job's task is to accept all that happens. Job seems to find this reassuring.

Has Job knuckled under to power, has he identified with the aggressor, as Anna Freud (1966) puts it? No. Job identified more closely with the aggressor when he thought he could put God on trial – that is, when Job thought that he and God were similar enough to be equal under the law. Rather, Job's comfort is similar to that of Elijah in the desert (1 Kings 19: 11–18), where God speaks not from the storm, or the earthquake, or the fire but rather from the silence that follows. God's silence, even God's absence, may be comforting – if, that is, one has once felt His presence. It is a presence that Job will never forget.

This possibility opens the door to a new reading of the strange and troubling conclusion (42:10–17), in which Job is restored. His brothers and sisters pay him tribute; he is given twice as many sheep, camels, oxen, and donkeys as before; along with seven new sons and three new daughters, each more beautiful than before. Is this just a mythic convention in which individuals don't count? Is this passage the introduction of a literal reward written by late and literal-minded redactors or, at least, redactors for the literal-minded? Perhaps, but something else seems to be going on as well.

Job has been on an incredible journey. Does anyone else in the Bible experience a theophany in which God explains Himself so thoroughly, but without an ounce of pity, as God does to Job? (Bloom 2005, 171). One imagines that Job is virtually incapable of elaborating his experience, virtually incapable of sharing it. There is a wonderful Greek word, *agos*, that may be translated in context as "this cursed, naked, holy thing." It is the term applied to Oedipus toward the end of *Oedipus the King* (1426), after his fate has become known to all. Job too has become *agos* – cursed, naked, and holy, all at the same time – a source of awe and dread to himself as well as others because he has gone beyond the human limit. It is likely that Job has fallen silent. What more is there to say?

For the rest of his days, Job will belong to another world, one that will not have him. So Job will reside in this liminal state, knowing the universe from God's perspective but drawing little comfort from this fact – indeed, drawing no closer to God. So, perhaps another reason that Job is given all of these worldly goods is to draw him back into the social world, to place him among all these living things (at the dramatic date of the Book of Job, before the invention of money, wealth took the form of being surrounded by living things, from slaves to sheep to generations of descendents), so that he might be lured back into the human world and not become like Oedipus at Colonus: a vengeful outcast cursing his city.

Of course, we don't know this. Søren Kierkegaard imagined that Abraham was depressed, ill, and isolated to the end of his days, just knowing what God had demanded of him, just knowing what he was prepared to do. "From that day on, Abraham became old, he could not forget that God had demanded this of him. Isaac throve as before; but Abraham's eye was darkened, he saw joy no more" (Kierkegaard 1985, 46). Job embraces his status as dust and ashes, his naked vulnerability before God – an exposure made more poignant as Job accepts (indeed, marvels in) the fact that he will never understand God's ways. What we don't know is how Job takes this knowledge with him back to the social world – the world of his new family, new wealth, and heightened prestige in the community. Evidently, we are to assume that he slips right back into the role of grand patriarch, but one wonders.

Perhaps Job has found satisfaction in abjection, in "living in the position of the dead," as Ruth Benedict (1946, 248–50) interpreted the Japanese expression. Perhaps we the readers have experienced vicarious satisfaction in that experience, for it is a space of strange freedom from the norms and expectations of everyday life. If so, then we must be allured and assured that the world of everyday life is worthy of a lifetime commitment. If this is true, then the restoration of Job is no mere late addition for the literal-minded. It is an essential part of the Book of Job, lest even the literary experience of abjection prove all too attractive, the call of the sublime a siren's call.

The dirty siren's call, it should be said, particularly in Kristeva's account. For there is nothing attractive about filth, excrement, or the corpse, all of which exemplify the abject. Nor is there anything attractive about the roots of the chestnut tree and the intrusion of the reality they represented to Roquentin. "This veneer had melted, leaving soft, monstrous masses, all in disorder – naked, in a frightful, obscene nakedness. . . . The chestnut tree pressed itself against my eyes." Escaping his categorization, representing "life in a particularly intensified form," the sheer reality of the tree threatens to overwhelm him, rendering Roquentin ill, nauseous, and abject (Sartre 1964, 127).

The dirty siren's call represents the same intensity of life, so similar to the *promesse de bonhure* on which Marcuse rests his utopia.[13] The promise is that of the lure of the original Sirens in Homer's *Odyssey*, particularly as analyzed by Max Horkheimer and Theodor Adorno in *Dialectic of Enlightenment* (2002, 46–8). It is the promise of the abandonment of self and its burdens; the promise of silence, sleep, night, of life at the edge of death. Here is the great virtue of abjection: it appeals to the desire for loss of boundaries and a return to the All, and it repels with its disgustingness. It is abjection itself – enticing us to abandon ourselves – that in the end repels us from its lure so that we might become individuals:

When the eyes see or the lips touch that skin on the surface of milk . . . I experience a gagging sensation and, still farther down, spasms in the stomach, the belly; and all the organs shrivel up the body, provoke tears and bile, increase heartbeat, cause forehead and hands to perspire. Along with sight-clouding dizziness, *nausea* makes me balk at that milk cream, separates me from the mother and father who proffer it. (Kristeva 1982, 2–3)

Released from his abjection, Job must be offered other enticements to remain in this world for as long as humans may, until he (and, more important, we the readers) is old and full of years, as the King James Version puts it, or at least as old as God and the Fates allow us to be. Why would the same enticements that work on Job work on the readers of the Book of Job? For the same reason that the clarifying catharsis works, in the same way that all drama, from Greek tragedy to "Days of Our Lives" (a television soap opera), weaves its spell: because the reader identifies with the protagonist. Without this identification, all drama loses its emotional appeal.

Conclusion: The Art of Being Humane

It is as a work of art that I have brought a psychoanalytic approach to bear on the Book of Job. I do not psychoanalyze Job and God; rather,

---

[13] Marcuse borrows the term from Stendhal.

I bring a psychoanalytic reading to bear on the characters called "Job" and "God" in the work of art that is the Book of Job.

The Book of Job has been regarded as a work of art in the further sense of being an act of katharsis, understood as emotional clarification and acceptance. The innocent and good suffer for no discernable reason, a problem made even more acute when one imagines that it is God who causes us to suffer. When we are confronted with this terrible thought (traditionally called "the problem of theodicy"), only the poetic form can save us. For the poetic narrative acts to hold and support us (and, in this regard, is akin to what Winnicott called holding, through which transitional space is created) as we learn the terrible truth. Poetic form allows narrative content to be heard and accepted, content that would otherwise be too terrifying to contemplate. Kristeva, Scheindlin, Winnicott, and Nietzsche in *The Birth of Tragedy* all made this argument, albeit in different ways.

From this perspective, art and religion are closely linked, more closely even than Sigmund Freud allowed. Freud certainly appreciated religious art, particularly Michelangelo's "Moses" (1914) and Leonardo da Vinci's "Madonna and Child with St. Anne" (1910, 107–19). In fact, this is Freud's point. Religious art is superior to religion not just because it reflects the artist's unconventional (personal, individualistic) insights into religion but also because, in doing so, art – like science – reflects the son's triumph over the father.[14] Religion, on the other hand, represents the submission of the son to the father, the ego to the superego. Otherwise expressed, the Moses of Michelangelo is "superior to the historical or traditional Moses." He is superior because Michelangelo's Moses is more clearly in rational possession of his anger, "an expression of the highest mental achievement that is possible in a man, that of struggling successfully against an inward passion for the sake of a cause to which he has devoted himself" (Freud 1914, 235–8).

---

[14] Like Freud (1910, 236–8), Kristeva privileges art over religion. "The various means of purifying the abject – the various catharses – make up the history of religions, and end up with that catharsis par excellence called art, both on the far and near side of religion.... That is perhaps why it [art] is destined to survive the collapse of the historical forms of religions" (1982, 17). Winnicott is one analyst who understood how much would be lost were religious belief reduced to the artistic katharsis.

If Freud's reading idealizes the artist, then we might ask – apropos of every case of idealization – what this idealization is defending against. Is there an experience that is less than or, rather, different than "the highest mental achievement that is possible in man," an experience that Freud would deny or cover over with his idealization of Michelangelo's Moses? Yes, and we might call it affliction, the experience of Job: that humanity was abandoned by God not long after the race was born, leaving us to be the dying animals we are, able to tell our own story – indeed, to render it sacred.[15] Not great art – in which the son triumphs over the father, including "our Father who art in heaven" – but rather humility, resignation, and acceptance are the virtues that will get us through this experience.

Art helps too, but intellectuals probably place too much emphasis on great art and too little on the art of everyday life. Part of this art is (or, at least, was before the mass media took it over) the art of storytelling, in which the community of those who listen is as important as those who tell the story. Together they – that is, we – weave a web of stories about our shared suffering, a fleshy human web that holds the children of our sorrows in a community of pain-sharers.

Think back one last time on the Book of Job and consider that it is not God who failed Job. God is God, not the mirror of human desires. Humans may be made in the image of the Lord (Genesis 1:27), but what that means is not for humans to decide, lest we indulge in the hubris of making God in the image of man. Or, as the Lord puts it elsewhere, "My thoughts are not your thoughts, neither are your ways My ways" (Isaiah 55:8). Nor did Job fail God. Job was resolute and, at the same time, capable not merely of learning but also of transforming himself to see his relationship with God in an entirely new light. About this God is satisfied – indeed, one might say proud (42:7–9). No, God and Job do not fail each other; every human, with

---

[15] Although man as a dying animal is an idea associated with Nietzsche and today with Richard Rorty (1989, 27), one might as readily associate the term with W. B. Yeats, who in the third stanza of "Sailing to Byzantium" refers to himself as one who is "fastened to a dying animal." The point, of course, is that Yeats, like the rest of us, might in some mysterious sense continue to exist when released from our bodies, perhaps in that form traditionally known as soul. About these things, it is difficult to know.

the possible exception of Elihu, fails every other human throughout the Book of Job.

Overly concerned with his own righteousness, Job fails his wife, Mrs. Job, who has lost everything. Mrs. Job fails to comfort her husband, criticizing him for his righteousness, advising him to "curse God and die." Job's three friends have the right idea at first, sitting silently with him in his despair; but, all too soon, they turn to justifying themselves and blaming Job for his troubles. One way to read the Book of Job – a reading not usually emphasized because it pays little attention to the great protagonist, God – is to say that if God is ruthlessly using Job to find a way to step back from His creation, then humans should be desperately figuring out how to treat each other with ruth – that is, with care, compassion, sympathy, and pity – because there will be no one else left to do it for them, no one to even set an example. Unfortunately, the Book's final scene (42:10–17), often referred to as "Job's restoration," returns Job to the social world but not necessarily to a more humane one. That remains to be accomplished.

3

Holocaust Testimonies: After the Silence of Job

Because Job never speaks after his theophany, we never learn if he ever thinks longingly about his first family while in the midst of his second, as some survivors do. Indeed, we never learn for certain whether Job's long life is a blessing or the curse Kierkegaard imagines it was for Abraham. Some survivors present us with a similar question. In some ways, it is *the* question, at least if we listen to survivors themselves.

A surprising number of witnesses say, in one way or another, implicitly or explicitly, that they "died at Auschwitz." Charlotte Delbo (1995, 267), a survivor who wrote several memoirs about her experience, said from the outset, "I am not alive. I died in Auschwitz but no one knows it." What could that mean? Especially for men and women who have gone on to marry (or remarry), raise children for whom they care and evidently love, dote on their grandchildren, and participate in their communities. One hears of this in numerous survivor testimonies.

There are, of course, variants. Max B. said, "I should have died at Auschwitz" (T-1125). Earlier, he said, "plenty of times it wasn't good to survive" (T-94). Several survivors wish they had died with their parents. "We should have died together, me and mother," said Eva L. (T-71). Martin L. expressed a similar sentiment (T-224). Rather than being a reflection of so-called survivor guilt, doubts about survival raise the very real question of whether the pain of living has been worth the price.[1]

Holocaust survivors are not the only ones to ask this question but the frequency with which they ask it so many years after liberation, often amid what appears to be a full life, is heartbreaking. Primo Levi's apparent suicide must be interpreted in this context.[2]

Few survivors commit suicide. On the contrary, Elie Wiesel seems correct in saying that the survivor's problem is not Hamlet's problem, "To be or not to be?" The survivor's problem is "To be and not to be" (Wiesel 1982, 54). But how in the world does one do that? How does one learn to live a double life, for that is what we are talking about and that is how several survivors refer to it. A strange double life it is, one in which the survivor's Auschwitz double never goes away, often growing stronger and more insistent over time.

The testimonies quoted herein are drawn from my research in the Fortunoff Video Archives for Holocaust Testimonies at the Yale University Library.[3] Several memoirists are also consulted, especially Delbo. Readers should prepare for some gruesome testimony. Why should readers put themselves through the experience of reading such horrific testimony? Partly to make a historical abstraction real and partly (more important) to point beyond the experiences of the survivors to the actions of the perpetrators, using the reflected horror of their acts in testimony to press us to ask the question "Why?" Why the terror, why the torture, why the torment, why the apparent pleasure in destruction – not only of people but also a people? I might have turned to Freud and the *Todestrieb* for an answer. However, like its

---

[1] References with (T-xxxx) refer to Holocaust testimony from the Fortunoff Video Archives for Holocaust Testimonies, Yale University Library, and should be read, for example, as Max B., Holocaust Testimony (T-1125).

[2] In *Primo Levi's Last Moments: A New Look at the Italian Author's Tragic Death Twelve Years Ago*, Diego Gambetta (1999) laid out the evidence for and against suicide, the alternative being an accidental fall. Not thoroughly convincing, Gambetta is persuasive in arguing against those, including Ozick and Wiesel among many others, who rushed to claim Levi as a victim of Auschwitz without knowing the full story.

[3] The interviews are not anonymous, but I follow the Fortunoff Video Archives' practice in referring to the witnesses by first names and initial of the surname. Most of the interviews I located on my own and many others with the help of the lead archivist, Joanne Rudof, a great resource. Others I viewed because I had seen reference to them in various texts, particularly those of Kraft (2002) and Langer (1991).

companion, Eros, the *Todestrieb* is best seen not as an answer but as a summation of all for which it stands.[4] Instead, I turn to the Book of Job and Thomas Hobbes's state of nature about which one can only conclude that it is a pleasant fiction – a picnic, if you like – compared to the regimes of terror that humans are capable of inflicting on one another. Testimonies are messages from the surviving victims of those regimes.

In addition to testimonies and memoirs, I draw on several studies, some of which are also based on testimonies in the Fortunoff Archives, such as Kraft's study (2002). The psychoanalyst who I find most helpful is Kristeva; whereas her work on abjection is the most relevant, I find her work on listening and love the most useful.

To Die and Go on Living

Among the most common phrases uttered by witnesses is the claim that "no one understands who wasn't there" (Sonia P., T-1681; Arthur R., T-2342). One might imagine that such a statement is prologue to criticism of an unknowing or uncaring public; occasionally, it is. More often, such a statement reflects the recognition that the witness has gone through an experience so unbelievable that he or she can hardly believe it. As Eva L. (T-71) said, "I can't believe it happened to me.... How can they believe if I can't believe?"

In *The Writing of the Disaster*, Maurice Blanchot (1995) was concerned with the way in which the disaster de-scribes, making writing and telling about it almost impossible. By *disaster*, Blanchot meant those experiences that disrupt our experience of going-on-being with the world, so that we cannot put ourselves and the world back together again (Winnicott 1958, 304). We cannot tell a story because we have lost the place from which to speak. That place is the present.

The disaster de-scribes because it destroys not chronology but the meaningful experience of time. This is what it means to "die at

---

4 For Freud (1920), the *Todestrieb* (i.e., death drive) was not simply the summation of human destructiveness. Freud theorized its existence in terms of a longing of the organism for the cessation of all stimulation, which he was led to posit from his encounter with the repetition compulsion, a quest "beyond the pleasure principle." About this aspect of the *Todestrieb*, one must remain agnostic. That humans love to destroy each other is easy enough to see; the source of this longing remains obscure.

Auschwitz" and yet go on living. One cannot have this experience without having dropped out of chronological time – that is, remaining frozen in time on the one hand, while continuing to live in ordinary, shared chronological time on the other, in which events such as Auschwitz are expected to slowly recede into the past. Only they don't. Or, as Abe L. (T-1394) said:

I thought that when the years go by, the Holocaust would go further away.... I dream about it. I can't get something like that out of my system. All gone now, especially the children. You can't get that out of your mind. The hole in your heart gets bigger. The Holocaust is getting closer not farther.

It is by no means obvious why this occurs, although many survivors refer to the increasing power of Holocaust memories in their later years (Fred E., T-664; Sara F., T-3022; Simon R., T-987). Robert Kraft (2002) studied the testimony of 125 survivors, concluding that whereas most memories change, memories of extreme trauma don't. The result is that the context of the traumatic memory changes because aging survivors now lack the distractions of rebuilding a life, raising children, and so forth. As Kraft said, "the power of distraction is most evident when it diminishes...a fading happier childhood, a decrease in worldly distraction, and the constant, laser clarity of the remembered horror combine to worsen the torment of traumatic memory" (43–5). Eva L. (T-71) said it more simply this way: "When I was younger it was easier. I was busier." To these reasons, I would add diminishing physical powers, increasing dependency, closeness to death and annihilation – all this intensifies the original trauma, which evoked similar experiences, albeit at the hand of man, not nature. Nevertheless, Kraft's explanation is striking. In aging, the problem is not so much that the traumatic memories grow stronger but rather that the forces that distract and compensate for them grow weaker.

Unfortunately, we cannot conclude that midlife is a time in which the force of the Auschwitz double recedes into the background. Even in the midst of life, the survivor is likely to be plunged into darkness and confusion by the most unlikely events. Consider the collision of frozen time with chronological time that Delbo experienced during the birth of her son. Ordinarily, birth is experienced as a new beginning: a new being is brought into the world and with it, the source of all that is fresh in the world is renewed. Delbo (1995, 261) originally experienced the birth of her son in this way but at almost "the very same moment as this sweet, enveloping water of joy was rising around me, my room was invaded by the ghosts of my companions":

I saw again this woman . . . lying in the snow, dead, with her dead newborn frozen between her thighs. My son was also that newborn. I look at my son and recognize Jackie's eyes, Yvonne's pout, Mounette's inflection. My son is their son, he belongs to all of them. He is the child they will not have had. Their features are etched over his own, or merge with his. How can one be alive amid these masses of dead women? (261–2)

How did Delbo manage to protect her son from the burden of all these dead women he seemed destined to carry?

The collision of dead time – or, rather, the time that belongs to the dead – and chronological time that continues is not usually so dramatic. In most testimonies, it is expressed in the witnesses' awareness that the temporal horizon of their memories cannot be contained within the conventions of ordinary chronological time.

For Lorna B. (T-94), "I could talk for days about one day in Auschwitz."

Sonia P. (T-1681) said simply, "Impossible to describe, all the happenings, would have to do it for days. . . . If you take it in detail, I could talk to you for years."

Simon R. (T-987) said simply (or perhaps not so simply), "I can stay and talk for twenty-four hours. You want me to stop?" Except it's not so clear why he asks his interviewers whether they want him to stop: For his sake, because he is becoming agitated? For their sake, because his story is particularly gruesome? Because his time is up (his interview is deep into the second hour) or because he (or they) wishes the time were up?

Finally (only there is no finally about it), there is Moses S. (T-511), who just won't stop. He is interviewed with his wife present and has told a particularly grisly story about eating a human hand in order to survive. At this point in the story, his wife gets up, saying, "We have to stop, I haven't had lunch."

The interviewer quickly changes the topic to "Where were you when you were liberated?" (a favorite safe topic for interviewers). However, Moses continues to tell horror stories, such as the night two hundred people were put in a freezing room, naked and covered with wet blankets. In the morning, they were all dead. He witnessed it all.

By now, one can hear Moses' wife in the background, among the interviewers and videographers, insisting that the interview be halted – for his sake, of course. Undeterred, Moses tells yet another story about how a Kapo killed a teenaged bread thief by placing a board on his neck and stomping on it, breaking the teenager's neck. Even as he is telling this story, the director is removing the microphone from around Moses' neck, the camera is turning away, and still Moses continues to tell his tale. We might consider the possibility that Moses is aware of his effect on his interviewers, enjoying a bit of role reversal, as in "Now it's my chance to inflict on you a little bit of the horror I experienced."[5]

Recall Abe L. (T-1394), who while crying softly through the last half of his interview, concluded that "the hole in your heart gets bigger. The Holocaust is getting closer not farther." Abe was not your ordinary survivor because he had left the ghetto and joined his brothers in the woods, where they met up with some partisans. "I walked ten days through the woods, crossing the river on a ferry run by a gentile in love with a beautiful Jew he was hiding. After I crossed the river, my new life began." For a moment, his story sounds like a fairy tale, but that moment passes quickly. At sixteen, Abe was too young to join his brothers in the specialized paramilitary units, such as the one headed by his eldest brother that blew up trains. Still, Abe felt the power. There were more than a thousand partisans at one point, enough to burn down cities, depriving the Germans of them. "We were in charge. Partisans had the upper hand and were able to take over small cities," even if they couldn't hold them.

One might imagine that activity rather than passivity – joining with his brothers, even in the role of junior partisan – would have mitigated the horror, the trauma of having life and death inflicted on him and those around him. It didn't. "Every night, I think of my brother's two kids, shot in cold blood by the local police." He cries when he tells about his grandmother, shot by a local policeman. The family was unable to give her a proper Jewish burial, so they had to bury her in the back garden. It is shortly after telling about this incident that Abe

---

[5] Langer (1991) suggested a similar point, I believe.

reflects on the increasing closeness of the Holocaust as he ages, and he asks that the interview be halted. He is one of the few witnesses who do.

One story neither proves nor disproves the psychological efficacy of action rather than the terrible enforced passivity of those who merely suffered the Holocaust.[6] Yet, Abe's story causes one to wonder about this distinction. Perhaps the horror of passivity so frequently associated with the Holocaust, the image of Jews being led unresistingly to their slaughter, has more to do with the fears (including shame) of those who came after than those who suffered the Holocaust. For those who suffered the Holocaust in and on their bodies, not passivity versus activity but rather loss – including the loss of everything that came before, above all the people, places, and routines of everyday life – was the overwhelming experience. Against this loss it is very difficult to fight.

Doubling

How do survivors manage to go on and live in the world among us? One of the most astute survivors said what she and others seem to mean when they say, "I died at Auschwitz." Asked how she lives with Auschwitz, Delbo replied:

Auschwitz is there, unalterable, precise, but enveloped in the skin of memory, an impermeable skin that isolates it from my present self. Unlike the snake's skin, the skin of memory does not renew itself.... Alas, I often fear lest it grow thin, crack, and the camp get hold of me again.... I live within a twofold being. The Auschwitz double doesn't bother me, doesn't interfere with my life. As though it weren't I at all. Without this split I would not have been able to revive. (Delbo 2001, 2–3)

In fact, this skin is not impermeable but rather porous, as Delbo's story about the birth of her son reveals. Doubling allows life to continue, but it is always threatened by the intrusion of the self who died at Auschwitz. Except that perhaps even "the self who died at Auschwitz" is wishful thinking, as though it were dead and buried. Even worse is

---

[6] In *Jewish Resistance During the Holocaust: Moral Uses of Violence and Will,* James Glass (2004) explored, through interviews with both Jewish partisans and concentration-camp survivors, the psychological effects of violent as well as spiritual resistance, seeing the sense of both.

the self who survived Auschwitz and comes back to haunt the self who would dare to live a normal life. More than this I cannot say, for it is not an abstract concept but rather an observational term.

There are no constants, no universal themes, among survivor testimonies. The two that come closest are "no one can understand who wasn't there" and "even today I live a double existence." Kraft (2002) argued that "doubling" is the near universal theme:

Almost all witnesses state that they live a double existence. There is a Balkanization of memory, where Holocaust memories and normal memories are assigned to two, sometimes hostile territories. . . . Consider a few phrases that witnesses use: "a double existence," "another world," "a schizophrenic division," "two worlds," "two different planets," "double lives." (2)

Needful of understanding is not so much the frequency with which witnesses refer to "doubling" – that is an observational given – but rather whether they are all referring to the same process, and what that process or processes might be. For some, the process is almost like that of watching another testify. "I made a videotape for my daughter. She said 'Mommy, you must be so sad.' But when I see it, it's like it happened to another person. . . . At moments you get mushy, but at moments you think you're telling someone else's story" (Sonia P., T-1681).

Reuben experiences doubling in a less literal fashion. A concentration-camp survivor, he speaks of himself as "like a *gilgul*," a ghost, a soul that comes back without a body to wander the world uneasily, lost. "Reuben's death" is how Henry Greenspan (1998, 66) referred to Reuben's life. Yet, of all Greenspan's *recounters* (his preferred term, although he also uses *witness* and *survivor*), Reuben lived out his days surrounded by the most abundant life: wife, six children, and a big dog with puppies wandering in and out of the room in which Greenspan interviewed Reuben for hours. Additionally, Reuben is constantly being called to the telephone, often, it seems, to settle a community dispute – a role for which he appears well suited but that is entirely informal. What to make of a ghost who seems so alive or, at least, so surrounded by life? Greenspan said simply, "The ongoing death that Reuben describes, therefore, should not blind us to the substance of his ongoing life" (67). For Reuben, doubling is a double helix, the strands of life and death wrapped around each other in a

complex pattern that in the end favors life over death, without ever
forgetting – or allowing the witness to forget – that every moment of
life is twinned with a moment of death.

And vice versa. By focusing solely on the living deaths of those who
died at Auschwitz, we "miss the vitality of their ongoing lives, memories
and legacies that have nothing to do with the destruction but which
allow survivors to recount at all" (Greenspan 1998, 169). This is what I
seek to understand – what is broken and what remains, and how these
two parts of survivors' lives live on close but not always intimate terms.

What is so puzzling about doubling is that everybody does it. Survivors don't double more than the rest of us; they double both less and
more. The self is always dual, as almost every thoughtful writer from
Plato on has recognized (Plato, *Republic*, 435a–443b). The cognitive
psychologist Ulric Neisser (1994, 8) stated flatly, "Memory is always
dual." He meant that the individual experiences the present self being
aware of the past self experiencing the world. The ironic quality of the
extreme trauma that induces doubling is that it results in what appears
to be an absence of the usual distinction (doubling) between what is
remembered and the remembering self. As seen by one who observes
the witness testifying, particularly the witness who begins to become
traumatized and overwhelmed as he or she recounts the experience,
the distinction between the "remembering self now" and the memories of the past self begins to fail. In other words, trauma is expressed
through an absence of ordinary doubling.

Traumatic memory has the quality of what Delbo called *deep memory*
(*mémoire profonde*). It is body-based, raw, visual, and expressed in
images, emotion, and physical sensations. These images are all too
readily reactivated, and when they are, it is as though the experience
were happening all over again. Expressed in simpler language, instead
of remembering the traumatic experience, the witness comes to relive
it. Or, as Bessie K. (T-206) said, "When it comes to me to start talking
about it, right away I step into the camp."

Delbo's deep memory has the quality of what Kristeva (1984,
21–106) characterized as the semiotic aspect of communication,
which Kristeva distinguished from the symbolic. Kristeva's distinction
between these two elements of signification is useful in clarifying what
seems to happen in the case of dread, the *angst* to which Kierkegaard
(1957, 38) referred: the presentiment of a something that is nothing,

an experience that is both nonverbal and nonverbalizable. As such, it cannot be framed and formed by the symbolic. Except in dreams, where the symbolic – freed of its usual grammatical constraints – mingles with the semiotic on a nightly basis. Both Kristeva and her teacher, Jacques Lacan, referred to this nonsymbolic element as the *real.* Unlike Lacan, Kristeva did not hold that "the real is the impossible" (Lacan 1977, x).

"Signification puts the subject in process/on trial [*en procès*]" (Kristeva 1984, 22). (In French, *procès* refers to both a process and a legal trial.) Kristeva meant that the signifying process is one in which the presymbolic (i.e., semiotic) elements are always pressing for expression, always disrupting the smooth, rational symbolic expression of the text or talk (39). The "trial" is really an ordeal (yet another sense of *trial*) for the subject: Can he or she allow the semiotic elements to have expression without being overcome by them? Kristeva seemed to believe that with enough therapeutic guidance and holding, the answer is almost always yes. Kristeva did not focus on Holocaust survivors.[7]

My research uncovered a puzzle. Many witnesses seemed to have extensive narrative access to what Delbo called deep memory, including what Kristeva called the semiotic, and yet this access does little to heal them. Rather, it was as if one part of the self could symbolically express the semiotic experiences of another part; however, the parts remained separate, evidently because there is comparability but no commensurability between the Auschwitz experience and ordinary experience, between the Auschwitz self and the pre- and post-Auschwitz self.

Think of the relationship between ordinary suffering and the suffering of the survivor this way. Everyday suffering, sorrow, and loss, which are enough to make a man or woman wish he or she had never been born, are nonetheless bounded by the forms and frames of

---

7 Kristeva (1996, 265) would perhaps disagree with my implicit claim that catastrophic experiences, such as those experienced by survivors, can reach back to destroy the archaic bond with the maternal object. The catastrophe can destroy everything, including the fundamental building blocks of the self. For Kristeva, this disruption – this affliction (*la affliction*), as she called it – seems to be strictly a developmental disorder, occurring prior to the acquisition of language (Kristeva 1989, 12–13). Or, at least, these are the examples she used.

everyday life: family, friends, routines, familiar places, the support of communities and loved ones – even as some of these may fail in misfortune and old age. All were systematically destroyed in the Holocaust: survivors were thrown into a hell of starvation, cold, and disease; surrounded by corpses, the caprice of death, and the taste of ashes; and, for many, the knowledge that their entire family had perished. For others, this knowledge would only come later. The losses of survivors are comparable to ordinary life; if they were not, we could make no sense of them at all. However, "comparable" does not mean "commensurable" on the same scale. Even the same words, such as "I'm thirsty," have two different meanings when you have been working in the garden for a couple of hours and need a cold drink, and when you have been riding in a locked boxcar with a hundred other people for days with nothing to drink but your own urine to wet your lips (Delbo 2001, 3–4; Max B., T-94). The fact that we have all been thirsty allows us to understand the thirst of the survivor; at the same time, however, it is a barrier to understanding.

Now imagine that this relationship takes place within the survivor as well, accounting for the survivor's inability to believe fully in his or her own experience. This would explain Eva L.'s (T-71) rhetorical question, "If I could come here and have a family and live a normal life, more or less, then how could it have happened?"

Doubling as the Loss of Value

In doubling, deep memory is cast adrift from ordinary or common memory (*mémoire ordinaire*) because ordinary memory lacks concepts and categories to explain a world that is no longer meaningful in human terms.[8] "*Warum?*," asks Primo Levi. "*Hier gibt es kein warum,*" answered the guard. When the entire world has no *warum* (no why), when the only answer is sadism, starvation, and death, then the self of everyday life possesses no resources to contain the experience, no moral framework by which to evaluate it, no chronological framework within which to say "this too shall end," no emotional framework within which to shield itself from unremitting terror and loss. The pre- (and post-) Auschwitz self lacks a sufficient vocabulary of value to communicate with the Auschwitz self.

---

[8] Deep memory (*mémoire profonde*) and ordinary or common memory (*mémoire ordinaire*) are Delbo's (2001, 2–3) terms. I use them roughly as she did in *Days and Memory*, her last book.

The experience of the absurd, which Camus (1942, 45) defined in terms of the gulf between humanity's demand for meaning and nature's unreasoning silence, takes on a strictly human meaning. Humans demand a meaning comprehensible to the pre- (and post-) Auschwitz self. The world of death that was Auschwitz replies with a meaning no longer comprehensible in the discourse of ordinary human life and death, in which death is measured by individuals, not piles of nameless corpses. Or, as Leon said:

> People hadn't become ciphers yet. They were still, up to that moment, human beings. With a name, with a personality. And when they were gone, their image was retained. But the mass disappearing into the gas chambers – they're just a mass of people going – like into a slaughterhouse. There was a difference. A qualitative and quantitative difference (Greenspan 1998, 159).[9]

The claim that Auschwitz had become the human absurd, by the way, would not fit Camus's understanding of the absurd. Why this should lead us to alter our understanding of the absurd is the topic of the second part of Chapter 4.

Shame is an interesting example used by both Plato and Kraft to explain the process of doubling (Plato, *Republic* 430a–e; Kraft 2002, 136). To feel shame requires, in a sense, two selves: one self has performed an improper act; the other self, in the role of judge, condemns the act as demeaning.[10] The selves are separate enough so that one can judge another, but both remain part of a larger whole so that when one self reflects on the other self, one self feels shamed by the other. The experience of the Holocaust, however, involves such separate worlds of value that the selves that inhabit them cannot communicate because they lack a shared moral vocabulary.

Consider, for example, the Greek mother who was told she could choose which of her three children she could save. Or the women

---

9 My argument seems to come close to Langer's (1978) well-known distinction between atrocity and tragedy.

10 One can see Plato puzzling over the divided self, for how could the phrase "master of oneself" literally make any sense; for if one is master of oneself, then one is also slave to oneself, and what sense does that make? Plato concluded that whereas the soul (*psyche*) of man is divided, there are better and worse parts; self-mastery is when the better part rules over the worse part (*Republic* 430e–431a). Similarly, in the case of shame, the better part of the self – in this case, *thumos* – becomes indignant at the baser part of the self (440a). If the key insight of psychology is that the self may be divided against itself, then Plato was its founder and chief systematizer in *The Republic*.

inmates who decided not to let the newborn babies and their mothers die, as the Germans wanted, but "rather that . . . we at least save the mothers (and kill the babies) . . . so, the Germans succeeded in making murderers of even us" (Lengyel 1995, 99–100). When survivors (and they would not be survivors had they not done so) make these choices in the name of survival, they are forced to violate their own most basic values. To live with these choices, they must double. The shame of this world hardly applies to the shame of the Auschwitz world, which would be to abandon the claims of life altogether and let everyone die.

Another survivor who was forced to violate her values to survive is Sara F. (T-3022). However, the term *values* makes it sound so abstract. It would be more accurate to say that Sara F. was forced to violate her feeling for life. Born in Lodz in 1914 and interviewed in 1993, Sara F. wore the brightest multicolored sweater I have ever seen together with huge triangular earrings. The impression is artsy, although her affect is depressed. Clothes seem important to her; she referred to them often in the interview. Sometimes they are all she can remember. For example, she can't remember if her first wedding was big or small, but she remembers her wedding dress.

Her mother and brother died in her room in the ghetto, a room in which five people lived at one point. Her husband was sent to Germany with the promise of work. He never returned. A Jewish policeman friend told her not to go, so she stayed with her friend instead. Later, she moved back into her house. One day, the police came and demanded that all the babies and children be taken downstairs. Once again, a friend said "Don't do it"; throughout her life she has not been without friends. The Jewish police came to her room, took her baby, and threw it in the wagon along with dozens of others. She never saw her baby again; no one ever saw their children again. Sara F. seems to remember best what she was wearing that day. For a moment, I thought she was lost in her own narcissism until she told a story about how after the war she heard that they sucked the blood from the children to give to the German soldiers. At one point, she seems to have trouble remembering her baby's name.

Sara F. is lost, I think, not in her own narcissism but rather in her own unnameable horror, still frozen in time. A friend of hers starved herself to death because they took her baby. Sara F. showed her work card, went to work that terrible day, and saved her own life. She tried to save her friend's life, tempting her with bread, butter, and onion sandwiches, but it was no use. Her friend died of starvation within weeks (neither Sara nor Sara's friend had been well nourished to begin with).

For the remainder of the interview, Sara F. talked mostly about people giving her things until that too stops as they die. After the war, her two sisters who immigrated to the United States prior to the war arranged for her to come to the United States, where they provided an apartment for her in a nice area of town. New furniture, new clothes, nothing second-hand or second-best – not after she arrived wearing a man's coat and a soldier's boots.

And now? "Now I have to see everybody dies." Her brother and sister died in the concentration camp. Her father, second husband, and just recently the second of the two sisters who set her up have died. "Now I'm all by myself."

She fails to mention her first baby and the son she had in the United States with her second husband, who is presumably alive – or, at least, she says nothing to the contrary.

The interviewer says, "Thanks for sharing your life."

To which Sara replies, "I don't know what to say anymore. I didn't do no one a favor, you know."

And that is the end of the interview.

One way to think about moral choice – for Sara F. made a moral choice not to die with her child but rather to live, eat, and work the day her child was taken from her forever – is in terms of what Nussbaum (1986) called the "fragility of goodness." Everything we value about ourselves – above all, our virtue, which philosophers such as Plato's Socrates took to be the untouchable attribute of the good man – is vulnerable to caprice, to fate, to severe and degrading misfortune. There is no untouchable core of goodness or virtue in any man or woman. If not social props, we require at least the maintenance of a decent social order, one that does not destroy us as moral persons by the decisions it forces on us.

However, this way of thinking about moral choice assumes that the severe and degrading misfortune we face remains on a human scale – for example, the scale of Greek tragedy, in which even as Agamemnon or Ajax or Oedipus might be destroyed, the values of the

civilization being portrayed remained. To be sure, there is irony here –
the values of Greek tragedy were the values of fifth-century Athens,
projected by the classic tragedians onto a mythic past – but the point
remains. The Greek tragedy that Nussbaum took as her model was
as much about the restoration of order as its destruction. Consider
what happens when every last remnant of a decent social order – a
social order built on the principle of life, Eros in its largest sense –
is destroyed? Then, one is faced not with the fragility of goodness
but rather "choiceless choice," as Lawrence Langer (1980) called it,
in which every choice is an insult to human dignity, every choice an
impossible choice: die with your child or starve yourself to death in
grief. Nothing you can do will save your child or restore a portion
of dignity to your child's death or your life. This was the situation of
many survivors. This is why it is so terribly difficult for survivors to put
the two parts of their life together again. How do you put together an
order built on death with an order built on life?

If Sara F. the narrator has in some sense been destroyed, her narrative has not. I use the term *some sense* in a particular sense: some part of
Sara F. has been destroyed; other equally real parts live, the parts that
have survived to tell what appears to be a truthful story. What is that?
Delbo (1995, 1) said it this way: "Today, I am not sure that what I wrote
is true. I am certain it is truthful." Sara F.'s story feels truthful in the
sense that Delbo seems to be getting it. Authentic to her experience
is a more long-winded way to express it.

Doubling is the consequence of the clash of values, although that
makes it sound too elevated, too abstract. Doubling results when a
world oriented to the values of life is conquered and overrun by a
world in which the values of death reign. To know something, you
have to have something to which to compare it (Plato, *Meno* 80d–
81e). If the new is entirely unrelated to the old, if there is no category
belonging to the old world that resembles that of the new, then the
new world will lack reality because it is impossible to find a place for
it in the story (narrative frame) of one's life.

Having just been separated from parents, spouse, children, and
home, the survivor is suddenly surrounded by the stench of death and
the taste of ashes. Starving, beaten, freezing, surrounded by walking
skeletons, waking up next to a corpse: to be thrown into this world of
death beggars the imagination. To continue to live in this world dulls

the imagination for any other during the time one resides there – and often for years afterwards.

"At Auschwitz, I saw more dead in a day than most in a lifetime. The smell of burning flesh...." Martin L. (T-224) can't, or won't, continue.

No experience, said Kristeva (1982, 3), is more likely to result in the experience of abjection – the symbolically uncontained and uncontainable irruption of the unbearably real into life – than to be confronted by a corpse. Many survivors lived for months or years surrounded by corpses, infiltrated by corpses, covered in their ash, taking in their ash with every breath.

For some, the smell never goes away. In the midst of her interview, Lorna B. (T-1126) brought out some burnt chicken bones from her purse to try to convey the smell of burnt flesh that she had lived with for months at Auschwitz-Birkenau, the smell that haunted her still every time she cooked (or at least burnt) the family meal. She was trying, with some success (to hear the gasp of her interviewer), to convey a deep memory, a semiotic experience. Yet, her success at semiotic communication did little or nothing to relieve her of its burden.

Another survivor put into words her experience of living with death when she said simply, "You're not supposed to see this; it doesn't go with life. It doesn't go with life. These people come back, and you realize they're all broken, they're all broken. Broken, broken" (Julia S., T-934; Langer 1991, 136).

Having experienced the unthinkable, many survivors can never quite believe their own story. They know it happened, but they can't quite believe it happened to them, even though they know it did. If this sounds contradictory, it is. It is the basis for doubling. Consider Eva L. (T-71):

The older I get, the more questions I ask. Why am I the only one of the whole family to survive? Who would believe if I can't believe it myself? When I was young it was easier, I was busier.... I can't believe it happened to me.... People ask me to tell the story, and I refuse. I can't believe a human could go through this.... Every day was a year. How can they believe a human can survive under this if I can't believe it? How can they believe if I can't believe?

Auschwitz for one who has lived inside it is evidently incomparable. Not merely the pre-Auschwitz self but also the post-Auschwitz self can hardly believe it. In a sense, this was the Germans' greatest and most perverse victory. They created a regime of death so horrendous that not merely those who were not there but also those who were can hardly believe it.

Doubling as Perpetual Mourning
The persistence of doubling is not explained only by the survivor's inability to translate between two separate realities, two worlds. The persistence of doubling is also an expression of perpetual mourning, a loss that cannot be worked through, a loss that is as real, vivid, and painful as it was fifty years ago in some cases.

Jean Améry (1980, 47–50) wrote that the experience of persecution was, at the very bottom, that of extreme loneliness. A profound insight, it is not alien to the concept of doubling as perpetual mourning, in which terrible experiences are experienced as the loss of all human connection. It is this loss that is experienced as death, as if there were no difference between one's own death and the death of everyone and everything one ever believed in and valued. Perhaps there isn't any difference. Or, rather, the difference is that from this death, one can go on living, including the lives of variety and richness that I have described, lives such as Reuben's or Primo Levi's. Yet, almost every survivor who goes on to live such a second life talks about a special sadness and loneliness that overcomes them at family gatherings. Indeed, for some survivors, such gatherings are terrifying, threatening to engulf them in endless sorrow. As Eva L. (T-71) said, "So hungry for family." She means, I think, "I'm so hungry for family," but the sentiment is so primordial that it is expressed as hunger in the absence of an "I."

Why? Not because Eva – and this holds true for many survivors – fails to feel a full measure of love and affection for and from her current family but rather because life is no recompense for her losses. The more surrounded the survivors are with living life, the more they are reminded of dead life, the lives that have been lost and the lost souls they have become as a result – Reuben's *gilgul*. It is as if every death has loosened their attachment to this world more than every life has strengthened it – just a little perhaps, but the cumulative effect is grave.

This is why, I believe, "I should have died at Auschwitz" so often takes the form of "we should have died at Auschwitz," meaning that the witness should have died there with his or her parents or other relatives. At least, in retrospect, dying together with one's original family, one's original loved ones, would have been the most complete life, the most complete death (Max B., T-1125; Eva L., T-71; Martin L., T-224). Except let us not forget that most who express this thought made, at the time, at least some small effort, and often an enormous effort, not to die but to live. Except who could reckon the costs of a life forever twinned with death?

Here is how the suffering of survivors differs from most who suffer from Post-Traumatic Stress Disorder (PTSD). As we think of it today, the person most likely to suffer from PTSD is a woman who has been beaten and raped or a soldier who has seen horrifying casualties on the battlefield, buddies being blown to pieces.[11] For many Holocaust survivors, the most traumatic experience is the loss of everyone who meant anything to them. Many came from small towns and extended families. For not a few, there was no place and no one to go back to and no one with whom to go forth.

Edith M. (T-4298) brought with her seven worn black and white photographs, which she held in her lap until the very end of a long (more than two hours) interview. Finally, in what seems to be a cere-monial moment arranged beforehand with the interviewer, she calls the roll of the dead, simply stating who each person in each photo-graph is for the camera. The camera lingers on each photograph for a long moment:

Her father, a handsome man with fedora and pipe, who perished (her term) while in the resistance in Bucharest.

Her mother, who perished at Auschwitz.

Her sister, who perished in the ghetto.

Two aunts who survived, along with their husbands and children, pictured with them, all of whom perished in concentration camps.

---

[11] According to the *Diagnostic and Statistical Manual of Mental Disorders IV (Text Revision)* (American Psychiatric Association, 2000), PTSD requires that two criteria be fulfilled (among others). First, "the person experienced, witnessed, or was confronted with an event or events that involved actual or threatened death or serious injury, or a threat to the physical integrity of self or others." Second, "the person's response involved intense fear, helplessness, or horror." The DSM-IV-TR criterion differs from the previous DSM-III-R criterion, which specified that the traumatic event should be of a type that was "outside the range of usual human experience." Since the introduction of DSM-IV, with its looser criteria, one study suggests as much as a 50 percent increase in diagnoses of PTSD.

Joseph, a first cousin, who perished in a concentration camp.

Her mother's brother, who perished in a concentration camp.

Several cousins and their spouses, who all perished in concentration camps.

Certainly, many survivors suffer from PTSD. Their tendency to relive rather than recall is evidence for that, even as it turns out that one can relive and tell a story about it (i.e., recall) at the same time. However, PTSD seems a pale diagnosis for one whose entire world has been depopulated – not merely of almost every person whom the survivor holds dear but also of the connections that constitute the fleshy human web that keeps us from endlessly falling. It is these connections that give the world its value. This is why phenomeno-logical or experiential categories, such as living after having died, or living a double life, or a ghost-like existence, are so important. In some strange and not quite arithmetical sense, these losses are additive.

In *The Nazi Doctors: Medical Killing and the Psychology of Genocide*, Robert Jay Lifton (1986, 418–29) characterized the doctors' key defense mechanism as doubling, the division of the self into two func-tioning wholes, each part acting as though it were virtually an entire self. Almost in passing, Lifton argued that doubling possesses an adap-tive potential that may be lifesaving "for a victim of brutality such as an Auschwitz inmate, who must also undergo a form of doubling in order to survive. Clearly the 'opposing self' can be life enhancing" (420). The trouble is, the way in which Lifton developed the concept of dou-bling reveals that it is not some neutral defense mechanism employed by innocent and guilty men alike in order to adapt to extreme circum-stances. Lifton's doubling serves death; the doubling I refer to serves life. The two uses of the term share only a name.

The doubling engaged in by the Nazi doctors worked something like this. Confronted daily with death on an unimaginable scale, the doctors came to fear death almost as much as the inmates did. To mas-ter their fear of death, the Nazi doctors gave themselves over to death, becoming angels of death, servants of the *Todestrieb*, as though they could master death by inflicting it on others. (Forget for a moment that the Nazi doctors were instruments of the death that terrified them.) Subjected to the starkest form of abjection, a world filled with corpses, the Nazi doctors sought purification through the infliction of death, the mimetic psychology of all purification ritual, as René Girard (1977) notably argued.

Mine is not only a summary of Lifton's argument; it is also an interpretation, one entirely consistent with Lifton's thesis. If so, then it makes absolutely no sense for Lifton to suggest, even in passing, that doubling, as he described it, is a defense that may be employed by survivors of Auschwitz, as well as by the doctors who experimented on and killed their victims. For the Nazi doctors, doubling was a defense that operated primarily during the years they served in the concentration camps, a way of giving themselves over to *Thanatos* (Carl Jung's term for the *Todestrieb*) so that that they might psychologically survive the world of death they were thrust into and made their own. For survivors, doubling is not so much a defense to be explained as a way of living after having died at Auschwitz. For survivors, doubling serves Eros, allowing them to live with what are essentially unbearable experiences. Both experiences happen to be called doubling; both concern Auschwitz. There, the similarity ends.

Religious Belief

Some survivors say they lost their faith and, since Auschwitz, can no longer believe. One survivor said that this is especially true of any who lived near or next to the crematorium, as she did. Whether that is generally true, I do not know. What Judy F. (T-211) meant is something like "we were given over to such unspeakable horror – not just death, for that's natural – but subject to such unspeakable atrocity, that the very idea of a God-ordered universe loses its meaning." What Judy F. seems to mean is a supposition; what Judy F. says is clear.

Reflecting on her naiveté on first entering Auschwitz-Birkenau, Judy F. recalled seeing a young Jewish girl like herself smoking a cigarette, and going up to her and saying, "Look, it's Shabbos. You know you shouldn't smoke on Shabbos."

In response, the young girl pointed with her cigarette toward the chimneys nearby and said to Judy, "Silly girl, it's Shabbos and look at all those Jews burning, their smoke going up the chimney."

About the young girl's cynical reply, Judy F. concluded, "Anyone would be bitter." Anyone includes both young Jewish girls that day and – for Judy F., at least – for thousands of days thereafter.

Others say that although they are not as orthodox as before Auschwitz, they continue to practice their faith (Daniel F., T-978; Ben N., T-358). Both were young men when they entered the concentration camp, and their lesser orthodoxy today may not be due to the experience of Auschwitz alone.

Some believe more intensely than before Auschwitz because it was there that they experienced salvific visions. Without exception, these visions are of relatives, never of God or His prophets, and yet the visions reinforce religious belief, although not necessarily of the conventional variety. When he was extremely ill, Jacob F. (T-120) had a vision that his dead father appeared to him and said, "It's a holiday, let's dance. It's Simchas Torah."

"Are you crazy?" Jacob replied to his vision. "I'm sick and defeated."

And the vision of his father said, "Dance, and nothing will happen to you."

"I danced, and then I knew," concludes Jacob simply.

Still others believe in roughly the same way as they did before they entered Auschwitz. For many, this means that practicing Judaism is more important than the particulars of believing in God. As Edith M. (T-4298) said, before she entered Auschwitz-Birkenau, Judaism meant observing all the holidays. Now it still means that but more: that her children are observant, that they all keep Shabbos, that all are married to Jews, and that her grandchildren all go to Yeshivas. Recall that Edith M. is the witness who recited the roll of the dead at the conclusion of her interview, beginning with her father with his fedora and pipe. For Edith M., her family's practice of Judaism represents not primarily a gift of the spirit but rather something equally important: belief in the continuity of life.

The one missing category is nonbelievers who became believers as the result of their Auschwitz experience. There is no one to fill that category; none in the testimonies I viewed, none in the memoirs I read – not one.

From the variety of religious experiences among survivors, it is difficult to draw conclusions, except that most witnesses do not refer to religion at all, apart from the fact that all mention (when it is the case) that they are Jewish. None whose testimonies I viewed fit into Levi's category of the true believer, whose "sorrow, in them or around them, was [theologically] decipherable and therefore did not overflow into despair" (Levi 1988, 146). Although it is difficult to determine, for I have only recollections to work with (for that is what testimonies are), religion seems to be most valuable in helping some survivors make sense of the lives they have lived since Auschwitz rather than helping them through the experience of Auschwitz, which remains a region of despair. Religion is primarily a source of continuity and connection between pre- and post-Auschwitz worlds. Not, perhaps, for Judy F., but even for Jacob F. The only time he smiles during the entire horrifying interview is when he speaks of the vision of his father inviting him to dance.

Yet, even the consolations of continuity provided by religion are threatened in old age, as doubts and despair too often return. Religious beliefs, it appears, are not immune to the fading power of distraction described by Kraft (2002, 43–5). Sara Botwinick (2000, 234) concluded her study of the impact of old age on deeply religious Holocaust survivors with this sobering thought[12]: "Even religious survivors may not be fortified enough to withstand the onslaught of invasive post-traumatic memories as they confront a state of increased vulnerability due to frailty and illness." From this statement, one might conclude that religious belief is a weak support. One might equally as well conclude that religious belief is a strong support, helping to sustain witnesses who suffered far more than Job (who, we recall, began to question God after only a week), without benefit of either theophany or a life lived in a God-drenched world. In general, however, religious experience seems not to be a special category of experience or belief when faced with the pressure of Auschwitz, even as religion proves for some to be a great aid in stitching the broken world together again after Auschwitz. Perhaps that is enough.

Love

About those arriving at the railroad station in the ghetto, about to be sent to Auschwitz, Delbo (1995, 4) wrote simply, "they expect the worst – not the unthinkable." Common memory can deal with the

---

[12] Botwinick (2000) did not refer to her subjects as deeply religious. That is my term, and it applies only in contrast to the convictions and practices of the witnesses referred to here.

worst; it has no place for the unthinkable. But, you ask, why doesn't testimony, putting words to the unthinkable, prove to be more helpful? Consider Primo Levi, who told his story so many times in both the spoken and written word and yet never could tell it enough. I say this not because he almost surely committed suicide but rather in light of the stanza from the "Rime of the Ancient Mariner," by Samuel Taylor Coleridge, that served as Levi's motto, the epigraph to *The Drowned and the Saved* (1988), his last book:

> Since then, at an uncertain hour
> That agony returns,
> And till my ghastly tale is told
> This heart within me burns. (VII, 16, 582–5)

Unlike most survivors, Levi could never tell his tale enough: enough times, enough ways, to enough people. No one exhibited greater mastery of the narrative form of Holocaust writing (such a form exists, and Levi was its master), but it did him little good. Or, perhaps one should say, not enough good (one might as well conclude that it bought him decades of life) because narrative is never enough.

In *Tales of Love*, Kristeva (1987, 277) wrote that we do not tell our narratives into thin air or to strangers on a train, as Levi did (Anissimov 2000, 257). That is, not if our stories are to relieve us of the dread that resides in the body of the semiotic, by which she meant something very similar to what Delbo called "deep memory." Only love provides the support to reconnect words and affects (Kristeva 1996, 121). Our lives have meaning for us not just through the narratives we tell but also through the narratives that are heard by those who love us. To be sure, most of the narratives that we tell others who love us never get told; we tell them to ourselves, in which the beloved other serves as an imaginary witness. However, this beloved other cannot be conjured out of thin air; he or she must sometimes play this role in reality or our narratives will become a story without an end, like a snake chasing its tail:

As we wander through our days, an event takes its significance in the narrative we construct for an imaginary conversation with a loved one as we are living it. The living body is a loving body, and the loving body is a speaking body. Without love we are nothing but walking corpses. Love is essential to the living body, and it is essential in bringing the living body to life in language. (Oliver 2002, xxv)

"Walking corpses" is, of course, a term frequently used for the inmates of the concentration camp, which shows that metaphors have an enormous range of signification, from the almost literal to the poetic and abstract.

Apparently, it is not enough for the survivor to be heard. A survivor wants others to feel what he or she felt and knows that it is "impossible to tell anyone how people can suffer," as Arthur R. (T-2342) said. It is a common sentiment among survivors. Sonia P. (T-1681) expressed it this way, "There is no way to make people feel what you felt." Sonia P. was a teenager when she climbed out of a boxcar window covered with barbed wire (her body still bears the scars), leaving her parents behind to die in Auschwitz-Birkenau. She was, she said, too young to die. She spent two years in hiding, in constant terror for her life and in constant guilt and mourning for her parents, whose fate she well imagined. However, she was not referring to her own experience when she said there is no way to make people feel what you felt. She was referring to a memoir of a concentration-camp survivor that she had recently read and how she empathized with his inability to make anyone, including herself, feel what he felt.

Because it is literally impossible to feel what another person feels, to what is a survivor like Sonia P. referring, to what do so many survivors refer when they claim it's impossible to understand another's suffering? In part, they refer, as Eva L. suggested, to their own inability to believe what happened to them, to their own inability to make it real, here, now. However, that is not the entire story. The feeling that one cannot possibly be understood seems to be a way of saying that no one can provide the living, loving body – to which Kristeva referred – the body that might finally contain the terror of the experience. Absent the listening, loving body of the other, one must forever be alone with one's terror, the point that Améry (1980) made when he stated that the experience of persecution is ultimately an experience of loneliness.

Are there other more spiritual ways of not being so alone? Telling the story of the Yom Kippur selections at Auschwitz-Birkenau, Daniel F. (T-978) recited a prayer in Hebrew, the same prayer that was recited by all the men in his barracks the night before the selections. Danny, as he refers to himself, recited the *U'Netaneh Tokef* (he did not give its name) first in Hebrew, then in English. "On Rosh Hashanah it is written, and on Yom Kippur it is sealed, who shall live and who shall die . . . who shall perish by fire . . . who shall be at peace and who shall be tormented." There was not, he said, a man in the barracks who did not cry. One imagines or, at least, hopes that for a moment each terrified man felt not quite so alone in his fear. The next day, many men were chosen for the gas chambers, but for the third and last time in his eleven months at Auschwitz, Danny avoided the selections.

The interviewer, Lawrence Langer, asked Danny if he sees a disparity between faith and the fate of these men.

"No," said Danny, "I didn't feel bad for the Jews who prayed but for the Jews who said to themselves they didn't belong there, who said 'I don't feel Jewish.' I knew why I was there."

Danny found, if not spiritual comfort, then comfort in his religion, for it helped him to know his place in the world even in Auschwitz. (I suspect, from other statements that he made, that Daniel F. was reading back into his Holocaust experience a later and deeper commitment to his identity as a Jew; but about this I do not know for sure. All research based on retrospection runs this risk.) In any case, one cannot help wondering whether some people are just better at finding comfort wherever they can. It is the same Danny, about fifteen or sixteen years old when he was deported from the ghetto to Auschwitz-Birkenau, who told the story in a previous interview given about eight years earlier, of making a friend of about his age almost immediately on his arrival in Auschwitz. He and his friend comforted each other, holding hands as they went about the camp, sleeping close together in the barracks, and so forth (Daniel F., T-153). It is difficult to resist the conclusion that understanding is an abstraction that rests on and sometimes desperately needs to return to acts of physical warmth and affection, but that with enough imagination, even God can be made to understand.

Dori Laub, psychiatrist and cofounder of the Fortunoff Archives, argued that testimony itself can have a therapeutic benefit (Laub 1992a). His prime example is Menachem S. (T-152). Confronted with the experience of witnessing, Menachem S. finally began to gain some control over a recurring nightmare that had afflicted him for decades. He was on a conveyer belt, moving toward a huge rolling press. "As I was moving closer, I would wake up, screaming, shaking, disoriented, couldn't go back to sleep." As a result of deciding to testify, he had the dream again, except this time, for the first time, he stopped the conveyer belt, and woke up anxious but fulfilled, not disoriented. "It has to do with decision to open up."

Menachem S. is a thoughtful man, so much so that Laub's co-interviewer, Laurel Vlock, said, toward the conclusion of the interview, "I don't think I've heard a more self-examined statement." She was right to be impressed. Only this is not an ordinary interview. In his essay, Laub (1992b) referred to an implicit "contract" between the interviewer and the witness:

> For this limited time, throughout the duration of the testimony, I'll be with you all the way, as much as I can. I want to go wherever you go, and I'll hold and protect you along this journey. Then, at the end of the journey, I shall leave you. (70)

Anyone who has seen the entire videotape, including the first eight minutes, which apparently was originally intended as a "warm-up," has learned that Dori and Menachem are friends with much in common. For example, both are child survivors of the Holocaust. Evidently, they spoke many times about Menachem's decision to testify (the dream occurred the night before Menachem gave his testimony). At a dinner, Menachem spoke with mutual friends about Dori and his work. Dori and Menachem are professional colleagues (both are medical doctors at Yale, where Menachem was on a fellowship) who expect to continue to see each other after the interview. Only when the "official" interview begins does Dori become Dr. Laub. In other words, Laub's prime example (indeed, his only example) is a witness who was in a continuing and evidently caring relationship with Laub.

One of the best pieces of evidence that testimony does not cure is repeat interviews, often after an interval of seven or eight years. In almost every case, the witness refers to how traumatic the original interview was, never to a lasting benefit. About his original testimony, Daniel F. said, "I did it for a lark. And I was depressed for months. I felt like I was back there. I really had no idea of what I was letting myself in for." This is from a man who had always shared his Holocaust experiences with his family (T-153, T-978; see also the repeat interviews of Max B., T-94, T-1126; and Lorna B., T-94, T-1126). Greenspan's extensive interviews over an extended period with a small number of survivors is another good source (1998, 172, n. 2). This is not to say that witnesses regret testifying; most don't because they believe they have an obligation as survivors.

This is what Martin L. (T-224) seemed to be referring to when he said, "Life in the United States isn't important. What's important is the ghetto and Auschwitz." At the same time, he already knows he will pay a price for his testimony.

"I saw Germans throwing babies out of windows in ghetto, people thrown out of windows, gives you something inside that breaks you down. . . . Couldn't do nothing."

Martin began the interview in control. An hour later he could hardly speak. "It's hard to talk about. The backflash before your eyes." He wiped his eyes.

"I saw people die by the hundreds."

The "fires are coming up, the computer is up" in his head, as Martin puts it, and all the pictures are in his mind. He circled around, but he couldn't find closure, a place to end, so he went back (the interviewer had the grace to not try to force the interview to a close) to watching his father's brother's children die of hunger in the ghetto. His memory is composed almost completely of visual images now – or so it seems to one who listens to and watches Martin's struggle.

Traumatic visual images are the most difficult to translate into narrative form. Images are not only the form preverbal experience takes before it is translated into language, but also the emotional trauma associated with these images tends to keep them segregated in the mind. Repeated enough times, these images-cum-emotions may be transformed into words and stories and eventually become bearable. However, it is a long process – for some, a never-ending process. Some find comfort in the process itself – that is, having someone to listen to the story again and again. Most find greater comfort in never reactivating the visual images in the first place – not if they can help it. The idea that telling the story once or twice could be anything but unsettling is, to put it mildly, naïve.

Martin went back to Lodz after the war and found no one. Neither did he find a single stone in the Jewish cemetery where relatives once were buried: no marked graves, nothing to signify a family member's existence.

Looking down at his hands in his lap, he said quietly, "So many dead . . . so many dead children. . . . Now I'm sure this [interview] will haunt me. My mother, father, brother, all their images come back."

If Laub was wrong that testimony heals, then I would be wrong to claim that every survivor practices doubling to survive. Menachem S. is an apparent exception to that generalization too, and there are others. In fact, almost any generalization about survivors is bound to be mistaken, for whereas survivors have much in common, they are not merely survivors but also individuals who survived.

Consider Edith M. (T-4298), the survivor who called the roll of the dead at the conclusion of her interview, beginning with her father with his fedora and pipe; the same survivor who finds comfort in the fact that her children and grandchildren display all the outward signs of religious faith. At the time of her interview (2004), she had recently quit her job in New York City and built a house on her younger daughter's property. Her elder daughter lives eight houses away, close enough so they can all walk to see each other on Shabbos. Born in a *shtetl* whose Jewish population was destroyed, Edith has done as much as she can to re-create what she has lost.[13] Does one focus on the losses she has undergone or the restoration of the remains of her life? Unlike Job, who remains silent, Edith M. gives us a choice, for she has told us about both.

It is not difficult to tell where her interviewer has chosen to focus. Almost before the interview is over, Dana Klein rushes up to kiss Edith on the cheek, exclaiming, "You smell good!" After all the death and ashes, even (or especially) an experienced interviewer seems immensely relieved to smell the odor of life. The trick, of course, is to find the life in death and death in life – the double helix of doubling.

As Edith M.'s story suggests, not testimony but rather the living relationship with another heals; heals but does not cure. Delbo (1995, 279–88) told a story about a peculiarly intense relationship involving a fellow survivor who found this living, loving, listening body in the presence of her husband. Without his presence, it seems likely that

---

[13] A *shtetl* (a Yiddish word) was typically a small town with a large Jewish population in Central and Eastern Europe in the years before the Holocaust.

Delbo's friend would have gone mad. After returning from Auschwitz-Birkenau, Marie-Louise could barely function, could hardly leave the house, couldn't speak to the postman, and certainly couldn't go to the market. Her husband, Pierre, who was not deported, not only took over these daily tasks; he became her second self. His most important task: to listen to Marie-Louise talk about Auschwitz for hours and days and weeks and months and years on end, until he knew her story and remembered the details better than she did. "We never stop talking about Auschwitz," said Marie-Louise. "My memories have become his own. So much so I have the distinct impression he was there with me. He remembers everything better than I do" (281). As if to prove it, she turns to her husband during their conversation with Delbo, who is visiting her friend from dark days, to recall various names, dates, and places when Delbo asks questions about what happened to various fellow inmates. Evidently, his memory of Auschwitz and after really is better than hers, even though he never left home. He has retained what she has been allowed to forget.

Today, Marie-Louise and Pierre are retired. They have moved out-side of town, which Marie-Louise found too noisy, and live quietly in the suburbs. Marie-Louise doesn't go out much except into her gar-den and to attend local and regional ceremonies honoring survivors. However, they have visited Auschwitz-Birkenau. There, Marie-Louise showed her husband where her bunk was, where they lined up for *appell*, where the men lined up, where a friend was shot, and so forth. This seems to have more fully enabled him to become her memory.

Is Marie-Louise fortunate? Perhaps, but in any case, few survivors will share her good fortune, a combination of her willingness to let another become her memory along with her husband's willingness to let his wife's legacy of suffering become his own. About all this, Delbo commented only that Pierre has a melancholy visage – but together, they hardly seem a melancholy couple.

It shouldn't be this way. Marie-Louise should have been able to retain more of her autonomy and still share her experiences. It hardly matters, however, for there are few spouses or lovers as willing as Marie-Louise's husband to take on the burden of another's memory and few survivors able to give up as much of herself (assuming the self is made of memory) as Marie-Louise. One might ask, however, whether what has happened between Marie-Louise and Pierre is the same as understanding. Understanding is not the same as identification. Understanding is an activity that takes place across an infinite gulf that separates you from me. Pierre and Marie-Louise have breached that gulf in the name of Marie-Louise's survival as a second self, but to say that her husband understands her is not the same. That takes perspective, and perspective takes a little distance.

Katharsis and Terror

Unfortunately, the alternative seems not to be genuine understanding (few survivors have found that – or so they say, and who else would know?) but rather living after having died at Auschwitz. Here, I include Reuben, who has become a *gilgul* – a ghost, literally a transmigrated soul living in another body, one that sets him free to move among the living by surrounding himself with life.

In experiencing these testimonies, one is reminded if only by contrast of the conclusion to the Book of Job, generally referred to as Job's restoration (42:10), in which Job gets back in spades all that he has lost, including a new family.

Is it a literal conclusion by literal redactors or (as I suggested) is it something more? Is Job surrounded by family as Reuben the *gilgul* is, so that he will not be overcome with despair and desolation? If so, at what? At losing his first family. If Job is like so many survivors, a second family turns out to be not so much consolation as reminder – or, rather, it is both. Would Job, like so many survivors, like Eva L., long most for his first family when in the bosom of his second?

One might also imagine that Job feels despair over what he has learned about God. Recall that Job's famous line at 42:6, "I despise myself, and repent in dust and ashes," might almost as equally well be rendered as "I regret what I have learned about God [and cover myself in dust and ashes in mourning for this knowledge]."[14] Job has learned that He is a God of awe and wonder but He is not a God of pity, not a God who cares on a human scale. Although it is the loss of family that drives many survivors to despair, it is what he came to learn about the world, and God, that seems to have driven Primo Levi to

---

[14] It depends on whether one regards the Masoretic reading as definitive, as pointed out in Chapter 1.

despair. Despair he expressed by placing Job as first among all books – not all books in the Bible but rather *all* books. Levi did this when he was asked to choose his favorite books or, at least, the books that have most influenced him. In response, Levi drew a diagram; at its apex, he placed the Book of Job (Levi 2002, 3–9). Read by moderns, the Book of Job states the human problem: how to live in a world in which humans have been abandoned by God. If that seems harsh, for Levi the alternative was worse – indeed, almost but not quite unthinkable: how to live in a world ruled by a malevolent God (more on this point in Chapter 5).

Other survivors lead us to reformulate the issue on a strictly human plane. (After one has viewed several dozen Holocaust testimonies, it becomes abundantly apparent that there are shared themes but only individual lives, and that many survivors build, or rebuild, lives more complex than any shared theme.) Consider Robert B. (T-1989). His interviewer seems determined to ask all the wrong questions, such as, "What was it in your safe, secure upbringing that made you so clever in surviving?" Robert B., however, wants to talk not about his clever stratagems to avoid execution at the hands of the rightist Hungarian Arrow Cross but rather about the cost of "the fear, the ongoing fear, this desire to be prepared for anything that could go wrong." It took him years to realize how crippling this constant readiness could be and more years of therapy to somehow learn to live with it. He is not vain or foolish enough to think he has overcome this fear; he doesn't believe he will ever overcome it.

Robert B., however, is self-conscious about what he would achieve with his testimony. He has a responsibility, he said, to relate the costs of his ongoing fear, this fear and terror of being destroyed: "Never knowing if I will make it until tomorrow. It stayed with me for years." Robert B. is not alone. Kristine K. (T-2687), a dentist who does not appear to suffer from PTSD or its kin, spent the Holocaust in hiding, including more than a year in the sewers of the ghetto of Lvov. Even today, she is like a starving person who sees the world in terms of food/not food, except in her case, the world is divided into place to hide/not a place to hide. Recently, she told the interviewer, she went searching for a new house with her husband. After looking at dozens of houses, they saw one in which entry into one of the rooms was through a doorway disguised as a bookshelf. They bought the house.

By sharing his terror and the toll it has taken on him, Robert B., like Kristine K., is allowing his audience to feel the *katharsis* of pity and fear in the sense that Aristotle intended the term (*Poetics*, c. 6) – not purging but rather emotional clarification, so that the audience comes to learn emotionally as well as intellectually what is truly pitiable, terrifying, and political: our utter vulnerability to organized terror (Shklar 1989). The term *political* is added to Aristotle's definition because it is implicit in his subject, Greek tragedy – public performances about the shattering of private lives by forces beyond our ken. That these forces turned out, in the case of the Holocaust, to reside within a group of so-called civilized men and women only makes their emergence more terrifying because, unlike the Greek gods, they surely remain close at hand.

If the function of tragedy is to accomplish – through the evocation of pity and fear – a "clarification (or illumination) concerning experiences of the pitiable and fearful kind," then most pitiable and fearful of all is the power of organized terror to shatter selves (Nussbaum 1986, 388–91). In *Nineteen Eighty-Four*, George Orwell (1949) suggested that contrary to their illusions, this power can work its way inside Julia and Winston so as to destroy them forever from within. This is the point of the last scene at the Chestnut Street Café (240–5).

This is what Eva L. (T-71) meant when she said that "At first, nothing could break the Jewish spirit. Nothing is harder to break than the Jewish spirit." She was referring to life in the Lodz ghetto. "We held marriages, Sabbath ceremonies, even with no food, and little bits of broken candle. We sang even if we hadn't eaten for a week." But slowly her spirit was broken. She saw her father swell up and die from hunger. (Eva L. cried softly most of the time she was telling her story.) Eventually, "that's all we cared about – more food for self and family. A human being changed into an animal." Eva L. is one of the witnesses who concluded that she and her mother "should have died together" at Auschwitz. Today, she says, she is always lonely – this despite being surrounded by a large second family.

This brings up another dimension of the Aristotelian katharsis. What makes the katharsis of pity and fear so powerful is how the katharsis is achieved. Through a process of trial and error, according to Aristotle, the tragedians came to learn that stories that involved the recognition of blood ties were the most likely to evoke these emotions. Stories of relatives thought lost and suddenly found, albeit not always for the better, are the stories most likely to evoke the katharsis of pity and fear (Aristotle, *Poetics*, c. 11, 13).

If so, then what are we to think of the stories of witnesses that frequently involve the recognition that all or almost all of those with whom one is bound by blood or marriage have been destroyed? When a survivor finally awakens from the nightmare of Auschwitz only to find that he or she has no ties of blood or marriage left in this world, is this a tragedy susceptible to katharsis or is it something else? For Langer (1978, xi–xiv), it was an atrocity; however, for Langer, the mark of atrocity is that the dead are nameless and faceless. For the witnesses, their dead, their relatives, will never be nameless and faceless; they are simply dead, never to be forgotten but nonetheless leaving the survivor alone in the world in a way that most of us will never be. Can we truly say that these witnesses have experienced a katharsis?

Of course not. Aristotle never imagined that the katharsis was to be experienced by anyone other than the audience and neither should we. The survivor generally experiences telling his or her tale as torment relived, not relieved. If there is any katharsis to be had, any clarification of the emotional experience of losing most of the links in that fleshy chain of human beings who connect us to eternity, then this emotional learning will have to be for those who listen to and watch testimony of survivors. How could it be otherwise? Aristotle was talking about a theatrical experience. Watching testimony is not theater, but it is still watching.

What do we learn? We learn that Hobbes was wrong when he said that humans fear their own violent death most of all. Worse is the fear that the entire world has been emptied of value, all human attachment, Eros in its largest sense; in this impoverished world, only one's body remains. This is not Hobbes's war of all against all, in which life is "solitary, poore, nasty, brutish, and short" (*Leviathan*, Part I, c. 13, para. 62). Despite his hyperbole, Hobbes imagined the state of nature as containing the foundations of civilization, such as families, which is why he imagined "the savage people of many places in America" as living in such a state (para. 63).[15] Not even family remained for many survivors of the Holocaust, who lived not through Hobbes's war of all against all but rather an act of organized obliteration, whose aim was to extinguish all evidence that a people, a *genos*, should have lived. For many who survived, it was as though the Germans had nonetheless succeeded, leaving survivors with insufficient markers of their own historical existence, their connections to the living and the dead. It is one thing to lose a loved one. It is quite another to lose everyone who ever knew that loved one, the cemetery where that loved one was to have been buried, the town where the cemetery should have been located, and on and on. Now, repeat this sequence with everyone that one has ever known and loved, which was the case for many survivors, and one begins to comprehend – if not the magnitude of the survivor's loss, then at least its arithmetic summation.

For survivors like these – survivors living in the position of the dead – a life of doubling until the very end is probably the best hope. Neither should we underrate this achievement. The creative ways in which many survivors manage to live double lives so that doubling becomes a double helix – life blended with death in the service of life, albeit a broken life – should not be underrated. At the same time, we should not forget that the psychological resources necessary to continue doubling frequently falter in old age. Or, as Abe L. (T-1394) said, "time makes it even worse." About some things, there is no better.

What about the rest of us, those who view testimonies, read memoirs, diaries, and the like, all to have some sense, however removed, of what survivors suffered? In other words, what of those who would experience some combination of katharsis and theoretical insight? What might we hope to learn? Not, I think, that we come to understand what survivors experienced. That is a false goal: first, because it is impossible and, second, because it is undesirable. Why should those of us who live comfortable lives far from organized terror (even as it is happening now in this world) seek to feel at one with its victims?

---

[15] Writing in 1651, Hobbes knew virtually nothing of the "savage people in many places in America" (*Leviathan*, Part I, para. 63). America as a primitive state of nature was an idea (or perhaps one should say a projection of the European mind), not an anthropological reality. The idea, in this case, is a society of patriarchal families without government to mediate between them.

Is that not an indulgence? (Weissman 2004).[16] Rather, we should listen to witnesses as though they were teaching us a history lesson. Not only or even primarily about survivors but also about their tormentors and the human willingness (dare one say eagerness?) to inflict suffering.

Consider Mauthausen (Mauthausen-Gusen) concentration camp, originally a granite quarry, established in August 1938 and populated with prisoners from Dachau, who dug the granite there to begin the rebuilding of Germany according to the plans of Albert Speer. More than any of the other camps, it is at Mauthausen that the Germans practiced extermination through labor (*Vernichtung durch Arbeit*). Estimates vary of the death toll from the entire Mauthausen-Gusen complex of four camps, with the average settling around two hundred thousand. Most inmates starved to death through work and disease. Two witnesses, Moses S. (T-511) and Jacob F. (T-120), referred to running up the same 186 stone steps, carrying 25-pound blocks of granite, day after day, season after season, often in temperatures as low as 20 degrees below zero, dressed in jackets and pants best suited for springtime. Both referred to the practice of guards playing dominos with the prisoners – that is, pushing the prisoner on the top step so that he would fall down, sometimes off the edge. If, however, he fell straight back, he would fall into the prisoner on the step below, and so on, each falling into the prisoner behind him. Many plummeted to their death together, some still holding onto their rock.[17] The goal, it is apparent, was not to maximize the labor output of the prisoners for the rebuilding of Germany. The goal, it seems, was rather to maximize the torture effect.

---

[16] In *Fantasies of Witnessing: Postwar Efforts to Experience the Holocaust*, Weissman (2004) explored how and why "those deeply interested in the Holocaust, yet with no direct, familial connection to it, endeavor to experience its horror vicariously" (from the book's front flap). As survivors seek unsuccessfully to unburden themselves of the memory of the Holocaust, some members of another generation act as if they want to experience it for themselves. This is one reason that sensitive interpretation of survivors' testimonies seems preferable to simply quoting at length. There is no entering their world; all one can do is listen and learn. I have found psychoanalysis as an interpretive framework helpful in this regard.

[17] These facts about Mauthausen-Gusen concentration camps in Upper Austria are well documented, including the 186 stairs of death. Weissman's (2004, 2–3) account of what it was like for a survivor to return with his son, only to find handrails on the steps to prevent visitors from falling, is both ironic and poignant.

One can hardly help but think of Sisyphus, condemned for all eternity to roll his rock up a hill, only to have it roll back again. Only Camus (1955, 123) told us that in the end, "one must imagine Sisyphus happy." Sisyphus has made the rock his thing: his fate belongs to him alone. For Moses S. and Jacob F., one can only imagine that Camus's essay must seem a cruel joke or a philosophical conceit.

4

Sisyphus, Levi, and Job at Auschwitz

What would Sisyphus do, who would Sisyphus be, at Auschwitz? One wants to say Primo Levi, but that doesn't quite work. Sisyphus, at least as interpreted by Camus (1955, 123), is the hero capable of creating meaning out of the absurdity of his own situation. This was widely held to be Levi's achievement as well. As one critic said, Levi's is:

... a triumph over the experience of Auschwitz.... Levi has given us the sense of what it was to survive, not as victims, but "as men made to follow after excellence and knowledge."[1]

The internal quote comes from "The Canto of Ulysses," a chapter in *Survival in Auschwitz* (1996), in which Levi struggles to translate a passage from the *Divine Comedy* into French as he walks through half a mile of snow with Jean, the Pikolo (or youngest inmate), to collect the day's soup ration for his work group. The publisher's blurb on the jacket of *The Drowned and the Saved* (1988), in many ways an even darker book, goes further:

A wondrous celebration of life ... a testament to the indomitability of the human spirit and humanity's capacity to defeat death through meaningful work, morality, and art.

---

[1] The same blurb from the *Chicago Tribune* appears on the first page of paperback Touchstone Book editions of *Survival in Auschwitz* (1996) and *The Reawakening* (1995). The latter book, written years after the first, recounts Levi's nine-month journey home from Auschwitz to Turin.

No wonder Levi's suicide was such a shock. As Elizabeth Macklin (1987) said in *The New Yorker*, "our fear was that the efficacy of his words had somehow been cancelled by his death – that his hope, or faith, was no longer usable by the rest of us."

There is no way around this fear and the demand implicit in it: that our authors live up to our needs of them. Today, there remains only the chance to reevaluate what seem to be discordant notes in Levi's narrative character – that is, the character that he revealed to the public as the narrator of his books. Not just in his books but also in relationship to his books. It is these pieces out of place that make Levi most real: the pieces that don't fit. If one reads a lot of Levi, including the interviews – which are also doubtless the product of artifice (Levi gave hundreds of interviews, perhaps a couple thousand; most are as polished as his essays) – an occasional odd theme emerges. One is his nostalgia (there is no other word) for Auschwitz. In several interviews, he calls Auschwitz "his university," and in an extended interview with Philip Roth (2007), he says:

I remember having lived my Auschwitz year in a condition of exceptional spiritedness... I had an intense wish to understand. I was constantly pervaded by curiosity... I suffered, but this was far more than compensated for afterward by the fascination of adventure, by human encounters, by the sweetness of "convalescence" from the plague of Auschwitz.

It is in this context that he referred to a doctor friend who tells him that all his remembrances are in black and white except those of Auschwitz and his return, which are in Technicolor™ (Levi 2001a, 17, 19).

Not all of Levi's friends, particularly those who survived the Lager (concentration camp) with him, appreciated his reference to Auschwitz-Birkenau as a "university." Ian Thomson, one of Levi's biographers, referred to his interview with Jean Samuel, the Pikolo. Only twenty-two when Levi met him, Samuel kept up his morale by setting himself algebraic problems to solve, going so far as to barter his portion of bread for a book on integral calculus that had somehow found its way into the barracks (Thomson 2002, 180–1). It was evidently this "sheer folly" that attracted Levi to Samuel, and they became friends in a place where friendship was as likely to bring jeopardy as mutual support. Although pleased to be visited by Levi and his young wife and daughter in the Piedmont during the summer of 1950, Samuel was deeply offended by Levi's use of terms such as *university, rite of passage, adventure,* and *nostalgia* to refer to their year together at Auschwitz (Thomson 2002, 262).

What in the world was going on with Levi? These are not the words of a man expressing what Roth called a "profoundly civilized and spirited response to those who did all they could" to eliminate his kind from this earth (Levi 2001a, 15). Levi's are the words of a callow youth (of whatever age) who has not yet come to terms with his own experience, whose works are more mature than he is – or, rather, whose own works are more mature than a part of him is. This would not be unusual, by the way; it happens with countless authors. It may be one of the best reasons to write, so as to live up to one's authorial self. Expressed another way, could it be that somewhere inside himself, Levi split his experience – or, at least, his representation of the experience – of the Holocaust? In this regard, at least, Levi would not be so different from Job toward the beginning of his spiritual journey, the man who rages at the same God he would have shelter him in Sheol until God's anger is past (Job 14:13).

Consider the dream with which Levi concludes *The Reawakening* (1995), his account of his almost year-long return from Auschwitz to Turin, first published in 1963, sixteen years after *Survival in Auschwitz.* About this dream, Levi's son Renzo said that if you read it, you will understand why his father killed himself (Gambetta 1999):

A dream full of horror has still not ceased to visit me, at sometimes frequent, sometimes longer, intervals. It is a dream within a dream, varied in detail, one in substance. I am sitting at a table with my family, or with friends, or at work, or in the green countryside; in short, in a peaceful relaxed environment, apparently without tension or affliction; yet I feel a deep and subtle anguish, the definite sensation of an impending threat. And in fact, as the dream proceeds, slowly and brutally, each time in a different way, everything collapses, and disintegrates around me, the scenery, the walls, the people, while the anguish becomes more intense and more precise. Now everything has changed into chaos; I am alone in the centre of a grey and turbid nothing, and now, I know what this thing means, and I also *know* that I have always known it; I am in the Lager once more, and nothing is true outside the Lager. All the rest was a brief pause, a deception of the senses, a dream; my family, nature in flower, my home. Now this inner dream, this dream of peace, is over, and in the outer dream, which continues, gelid, a well-known voice resounds: a single word, not imperious, but brief and subdued. It is the dawn command of Auschwitz, a foreign word, feared and expected: get up, "*Wstawàch*." (Levi 1995, 207–8)

About Renzo Levi's interpretation, one can do more than sympathize; one can say that it makes sense of Levi's suicide.

What doesn't make sense is the concluding footnote to the Italian scholastic edition of *The Reawakening*, which referred to this passage. (The original Italian is *La Tregua* [The Truce], which seems more accurate, suggesting an interval, not a rebirth.) There, Levi argued that the Lager has universal significance, having become the symbol of the human condition – that is, mortality. The feared voice in Polish, get up, "*Wstawàch*," is the voice that leads to death. Death is inscribed in life:

> . . . possessing a power in a way no different from that power it was impossible to disobey on cold mornings at Auschwitz. . . . The Lager is always, constant and eternal. What may change is only the place in which one experiences it.[2]

This is not only nonsense; it is confused and confusing nonsense, for in the end it confounds life and death.

All of life is not the Lager and all of life does not aim to end in the Lager, which represents not just death but also the humiliation and obliteration of individuals so that no trace and no memory remain. One thinks here of a post-Holocaust Solomon (Kohelet).[3] One who has become so world-weary that he can see no difference between a humiliating and obliterating death in the Lager and a dignified death (or perhaps this is an idealization, so let us say merely a human death) at the end of a long life in the company of family and friends. That too may be an idealization in today's medicalized world of death and dying, but it is not an impossibility. Having recently attended the death of a friend, I know. Our Solomon, however, has become so world-weary that it seems he has trouble making a distinction between living and dying in a manmade hell and living and dying a natural death in a human world.

---

[2] This is Patruno's (1995, 53, and note 27) gloss on Levi's footnote to the Einaudi series, "Letture per la scuola media," no. 3, rpt. 1986, 269–70.

[3] The noun *Kohelet*, applied to the author, said to be King Solomon (which is unlikely because the text seems to date from a more recent era), is often translated as speaker or student (as in student of Solomon). Some hold it to be a proper name.

Recall a theme running through the Book of Job, in which God's ability to impose suffering and death is the surest sign of His living presence, a sign that He is still involved in the process of creation. The result is an almost inevitable tendency to confuse creation and destruction. Is not Levi similarly confused when he argued not merely that the Lager is a metaphor for the human condition but also that "we are all in the ghetto, that the ghetto is walled in, that outside the ghetto reign the lords of death, and that close by the train is waiting" (1988, 69).

Levi made these comments about the Lager and the ghetto in the last years of his life, when he was sick and depressed. (*The Reawakening* was published years before, but the notes to the scholastic edition [*Letture per la scuola media*] were published in 1986.) One wonders if Levi's depression, from which he evidently suffered for years, coupled with his experience of living again so close to death, trapped in the same apartment with his dying mother (whose skeletal body, he said, reminded him of the dying inmates at Auschwitz[4]), led him to an especially cynical view of death, in which one death is as meaningless as another. Or, was Levi like several older survivors whose testimonies were quoted in the previous chapter? For these aging survivors, Auschwitz seemed to come closer in the last years, as the distractions of everyday life and work receded, accompanied by an awareness of the body's increasing weakness and vulnerability, possibly reminding the survivor of prior periods of desperate exposure and need.

Why Levi transformed the concentration camp and ghetto into metaphors for the human condition must remain speculation. It deserves to be stated clearly that he was wrong. There is a vast difference between the ghetto created by the Nazis to collect, weaken, and torment its victims before sending them to their destruction and the communities in which some of us are privileged to live. Communities in which the cycle of life and death is not a degrading experience imposed by other humans but rather a natural event in which humans, when fortunate, are comforted by the presence of children

---

[4] From Anissimov (2000, 405). There is some question about whether Levi made this statement about his mother reminding him of the dying inmates at Auschwitz (see note 10 and corresponding text). There is no doubt that he felt trapped with his dying mother.

and grandchildren who will carry on some of their hopes and dreams (not all, for each generation belongs to itself) rather than being extinguished along with them, so that no one is left to carry on. Indeed, no one is left who even remembers. That is the horror of genocide. These are, needless to say, hardly trivial distinctions.

Yet, in the end, it is not Levi's life that disqualifies him for the role of Sisyphus in Auschwitz. It is Levi's own teachings, which draw others into the story, albeit only at an artist's distance – the distance needed to observe others closely but not close enough to become deeply attached. At least, that is the impression Levi leaves. Sisyphus was always alone. About how best to depart Auschwitz alive, Levi gave the following advice: "How was I able to survive in Auschwitz? My principle is: I come first, second, and third. Then nothing, then again I; and then all the others" (Levi 1988, 79).[5] Those who survived in this way Levi called "the saved." The result, said Levi, was a type of reverse moral Darwinism in the camps, "the survival of the worst," as slyness and deceit gave one a better chance of survival than did bravery (Patruno 1995, 121).

Others simply gave up all hope and abandoned the struggle for survival altogether. "The drowned," Levi called them, and for Levi they were not really men at all; they were already dead, without merit, dignity, or human value. Most abandoned the struggle to survive not out of a higher value but rather because they were weak, foolish, or stupid. About these men, Levi said that he did virtually nothing to comfort them. Any assistance he could have offered would have been useless to them, and it would have distracted him from the task of furthering his own survival, a task that occasionally included cultivating *protekcja*, or privileged ones (Levi 2001b, 39). I say this not to detract from Levi. On the contrary, he was admirably honest about his own behavior, and quite unwilling to judge – indeed, he frequently absolved – those whose behavior was the result of the constraints of survival (Levi 1988, 44). I say this only because Levi's claim that morality did not apply in the Lager, not even to himself, is often overlooked, as though Levi were only being polite to include himself

---

5 Levi was using the words of another to explain his own position. His practice was often different. Levi had friends at Auschwitz, sometimes practicing a type of selfishness that he (1988, 80) called us-ism.

among those determined and desperate enough to do almost anything (but not anything: Levi would not steal another's portion of food) to survive.

The drowned and the saved lived together in a world in which even the strongest will to survive meant little: not nothing, but far less than the forces of caprice that ruled the world of the Lager. However, calling it caprice renders these forces too abstract. All inmates lived under a sentence of death, doled out in daily portions by men and women who may not have been devils but who willingly accepted the role for the duration. Relatively few inmates managed to survive long enough until the devils were driven out of hell. Here is the moral message of Primo Levi:

It is naïve, absurd, and historically false to believe that an infernal system such as National Socialism was, sanctifies its victims; on the contrary, it degrades them, it makes them similar to itself. (1988, 40)[6]

This is not the entire message, to be sure, but the message that is at the core of his writings. Blanchot (1995, ix) referred to knowledge of the disaster having become "knowledge as disaster." One can say this both about Levi's teachings and, in all likelihood, his life. Another way of expressing it is that Levi was insufficiently talented at doubling; he lived too close to the disaster. Levi succumbed to "the danger that the disaster acquire meaning instead of body," as Blanchot (1995, 41) stated. By "body," Blanchot meant something like what Kristeva (1987) meant in *Tales of Love*.

Levi and Job

Finally, consider Levi's few, brief, but always important references to the Book of Job – in this case, in a commentary on the television series "Holocaust," which on the whole he found admirable. Hundreds of calls besieged the broadcasting station in the countries where the film

---

[6] Levi continued, "and this all the more when they are available, blank, and lack a political or moral armature." Although the final qualifying clause is significant, it applied to a relatively few inmates: those who entered the camps with deep religious or political convictions, such as Ezra, the cantor who fasted on Yom Kippur, baffling the Kapo in charge, who had never seen such a thing (Levi 1988, 40–41). The everyday religious or political beliefs of the majority provided no support at all.

was shown and, for the most part, the viewers wanted to know one thing: Why?

And this is a huge "why," as ancient as humankind itself. It is the why of the evil of the world, the why that Job futilely addresses to God, and which we can answer with a number of half answers: but the global, universal answer, the one to bring peace to the spirit, is unknown and perhaps does not exist. (Levi 2005, 61–2)

There is much to say about this seemingly simple and sensible answer. First, it is not clear what Levi meant by the "global, universal answer" except that he seems to equate it with an answer that brings "peace to the spirit." It may be that there is an answer, one that includes both God and evil in the same equation but does not bring peace to the spirit – or, at least, not unalloyed peace – but a much more complex ensemble of emotions.

Job, conversely, does find something akin to the peace to which Levi referred, and it is indeed connected to his discovery of a global, universal answer. And what is that? That there is no answer. To even ask the classical question of theodicy, "Why do the innocent suffer if God is all good and all powerful?," is to misunderstand one's place in the universe. To ask this question is already to put the Lord on trial. To ask this question is already to participate in Job's hubris (before his encounter with the Lord of the whirlwind). The only attitude proper to humans when faced with the inexplicable, the morally outrageous, the unbearably sad, is acceptance.

God has ordered the world so that there is sense to even the most senseless experiences, such as the death of a child (or, one must say it, millions of children). Humans, however, will never understand this order unless God chooses to reveal it to us, and so we must have faith. This is the message of the Book of Job: God reveals to Job the magnificence of His creation, thereby demonstrating the existence of an ordering principle to the universe. This is simple fact, at least for Job. What remains obscure is the content of this principle. Accepting this obscurity, which is tantamount to accepting that human knowledge is powerless before the most important questions – the questions that quake us to the bone – means that one can finally achieve the peace of the spirit that Job achieves. Not the peace of Job's "restoration," as it is called, but the peace that settles on Job when he takes comfort in his dust and ashes – that is, his mortality, the fact that he is nothing more than one more creation of his Lord, and nothing less.

In *The Search for Roots* (*La ricera delle radici*, first published in 1981), Levi collected thirty passages from literary and nonliterary authors, each passage preceded with a brief introduction by Levi (2002). It would not seem an especially personal or revealing book. Yet, it is about this book that Levi said, "I have never exposed myself more fully to my readers than in making the choice of these excerpts. Much more than in writing my books. Halfway through, I felt completely naked" (2002, 5). One might read this surprising statement as suggesting how little Levi exposed of himself in his memoirs. The narrator of *Survival in Auschwitz, The Reawakening, The Drowned and the Saved,* and other works is a man called Primo Levi, but he is not Primo Levi the man. The narrator is Primo Levi the artifice, creation of the author. About the man we know little and think we know much. In an "Introduction" to his translation of *The Search for Roots*, Peter Forbes said:

Many readers, of course, see Primo Levi himself as an exceptional case of the reliable narrator – what Levi says of Rigoni Stern applies equally well to himself: "It is rare to find such an accord between the man who lives and the man who writes." (2002, xii)

This is the artifice, still working its magic. In what does the magic consist? In leading us to move from the first assertion to the second. Levi *is* a reliable narrator; he is the great truth teller about the Holocaust and all that it represents. What this does not mean is that the man and the writer are one. Even so, they cannot be completely separate, as a thought experiment by Berel Lang (2000, 79–81) revealed.

Imagine that after his death, a letter from Levi was found saying that he was not the author of the works that bear his name. He escaped from the train taking him to Auschwitz, sat out the war in the mountains of Northern Italy, and there met a man whose extraordinary stories seemed to come from life, not just his but also others. Levi "transcribed" these stories and left this duly notarized letter to be opened after his death. What difference would it make? All the difference in the world. The demand for transparency, in the end, may be seen as a demand that we not be tricked: not just about the author but also about the facts (in writing about the Holocaust, no other word will do) about which he writes. This, at least, is what the legitimate demand for authorial transparency reflects. In Levi's case, the demand is for more – more than Levi could sustain, more than is fair to ask: that he remain untouched, undamaged by the Holocaust in the deepest places of his soul.

The selections (all abridged) in *The Search for Roots* are arranged in no clear order, so at the end of his preface, Levi provided a diagram suggesting "four possible routes through some of the authors in view" (2002, 8). The diagram, "the most important page in the book," according to Italo Calvino (2002, 222), displays an ovoid sphere with four meridians, each representing alternative literary paths from north to south. At the North Pole is Job. "To Job I have instinctively reserved the right of primogeniture," wrote Levi (2002, 8). The South Pole is called "Black Holes" (*Buchi Neri*), a theme, or rather trope, that was to become increasingly important in Levi's later work. The book's last essay is an article on Black Holes from *Scientific American*, to which Levi has given the title "We Are Alone." Connecting the poles are authors who influenced Levi, authors as diverse as Rabelais, T. S. Eliot, Paul Celan, Marco Polo, Sholem Aleichem, Joseph Conrad, and Charles Darwin. For now, I am interested only in what Levi said about Job and Black Holes:

The Book of Job has been chosen in order to confront the existence of evil in the world. Job is the just man crushed by injustice. He is the victim of a cruel wager between Satan and God....Job, the just man humbled like an animal, as usual behaves as any of us would. At first he bows his head and praises God....Then his defenses crumbled. Poor, robbed of his children, covered in boils, he sits among the ashes, scraping himself with a potsherd, and argues with God. It is an unequal argument. God the creator of marvels and monsters crushes him beneath his omnipotence. (2002, 11)[7]

There are other ways to read the Book of Job. Absent any sophisticated reading, we already know that Levi regarded Job's encounter with the Lord of the whirlwind as signifying little more than God lording it over Job. The way Levi chose to read it is compatible with an interpretation that suggests how easy it would be for the author to

---

[7] I cite the English translation but use Anissimov's (1999, 182) translations of the extended quotation from *The Search for Roots*. Her translation emphasized Levi's confrontation with the question of theodicy.

move directly from the Book of Job to Black Holes, from evil to oblivion, from the cry for justice that goes unanswered to being swallowed by the endless night.

About Black Holes, Levi said that every year that passes leaves us more alone in the universe, the result of new scientific discoveries in astronomy and astrophysics:

Not only are we not the center of the universe, but the universe is not made for human beings; it is hostile, violent, alien. In the sky there are no Elysian Fields, only matter and light. (2002, 214)

Marcuse (1978, 69) made a similar comment about the world not being made for the sake of the human being. Yet, Marcuse's tone is different. Marcuse was a utopian, one who understands the enormous social transformation necessary to make this world a fit one for human beings. Levi concluded with a remarkably naïve comment:

Perhaps we are the sole instance of intelligence in the universe; certainly we are immeasurably small, weak and alone, but if the human mind has conceived Black Holes, and dares to speculate on what happened in the first moments of creation, why should it not know how to conquer fear, poverty, and grief? (2002, 214–15)

Is the simple answer not the best? We know how to conquer the worst forms of poverty but are not willing to make the collective sacrifice. About the two end terms, *fear* and *grief*, they will presumably always be with us because they are a large part of what it means to live a human life on this planet. What must be distinguished and fought against, following Marcuse, is what might be called the "surplus" forms of all three: that measure of poverty, fear, and grief that is not intrinsic to the human condition but rather serves to maintain or express hierarchies of wealth, power, and domination. More on this point shortly.

Thomson (2002, 528) suggested that the increasing frequency of Black Holes in Levi's later work expresses his depression and presages his suicide. Consider the leading lines of the essay that Levi chose to conclude *The Search for Roots*, lines that refer to "a hole in space with a definite edge over which anything can fall and nothing can escape; a hole with a gravitational field so strong that . . . [it] warps time" (2002, 215). How easy to read this passage as metaphor for the gravitational pull of the semicircular stairwell in his apartment building from which

Levi almost surely jumped.[8] The stairwell, described by one who visited Levi's third-floor apartment as giving the "giddy sensation of a spiral void," had evidently long exercised its pull on Levi's imagination (Thomson 2002, 531). For sixty-five of his sixty-seven years, Levi lived at the edge of that stairwell. At more than one point in his work, Levi compared death to jumping off the third floor.[9] In a late short story, "Westward," one of the characters who is studying the collective suicide of lemmings refers to her own postnatal depression as "that hole, that void" (Anissimov 2000, 309–10). Of course, this is not an unusual way to refer to depression, and we know that Levi was depressed.

Drawn by his own declining health, as well as the almost cadaverous state of his severely ill mother, was Levi not caught in a time warp of his own? About his mother, Levi said:

I don't know how I can go on. I can't stand this life any longer. My mother has cancer, and each time I look at her face I remember the faces of the men lying dead on the planks of the bunks in Auschwitz. (Anissimov 2000, 405)[10]

Indeed, Levi said that his last years were in some respects worse than Auschwitz, for he was older and lacked the strength to resist. Resist what? His letter to his translator, Ruth Feldman, doesn't entirely answer the question. "I'm going through my worst time since Auschwitz: in certain respects it's even worse than Auschwitz, because I'm no longer young and have scant resilience. My wife is exhausted" (Thomson 2002, 527–8).

---

[8] "Semicircular" is imprecise. Gambetta (1999) said that "horizontally, it is shaped like a cut-off pyramid."

[9] Levi 1996, 160, "more surely fatal than jumping off a fourth floor." In Europe, the first floor is the ground floor. Levi lived on and jumped or fell from his third floor, "our" fourth floor (Thomson 2002, 531). Levi was born and died in the same apartment building; his writing desk was said to be situated where the bed on which he was born was once located. Except for the almost two years he spent in an internment camp, Auschwitz-Birkenau, and his long return home, Levi spent his entire life at 75 Corso Re Umberto.

[10] This quotation from Levi comes from Elio Toaff, Chief Rabbi of Rome, who claims that Levi said these words to him in a telephone call "ten minutes before" he died. The Rabbi, who had never met Levi, only disclosed their conversation on the tenth anniversary of Levi's death. Levi died on a Saturday and, as Gambetta (1999) pointed out, it is unlikely that an orthodox Rabbi would answer the telephone on a Saturday. Of course, the Rabbi could misremember the day (perhaps it was Friday morning: Levi died shortly before ten) but still accurately remember the conversation.

To fellow writer and survivor, Edith Bruck, Levi said, "It was better at Auschwitz. At least then I was young, and believed" (Angier 2002, 713). Believed in what? Levi was not likely referring to God here. Angier suggested the following possibilities: man, reason, the possibility of understanding. To this, I would add the most important of all: the possibility of being understood – that is, the possibility of communicating his experience to others. Nothing was ever more important to Levi.

How important are these insights into Levi's life? In one respect, they are not important at all. While it would be a mistake to claim that his work speaks for itself (no work does that), the narrative voice known as Primo Levi sees the world clearly enough, making few enough missteps along the way, that we can learn from him without having to distinguish the man from the voice. In other words, there is more to learn from the lecture than the lecturer. Nevertheless, Levi wrote primarily in the style of the memoirist, and there remains a darkness in Levi's heart that was not fully explained by the self-restraint engendered by his insight that an author's feelings will not necessarily be echoed by his readers.

I believe that this darkness is best explained by the distinction between the torment of Job and that of Levi, and that this distinction roughly tracks the distinction between affliction and abjection. Affliction is suffering made meaningful because it takes place within a larger world of meaning. How large must this world be: as large as the universe or "merely" the extended human family? The question remains unanswered – not unanswerable, simply without an answer in principle.

Abjection stems from the irruption of the unbearably real into a life in such a profound, overwhelming, and terrifying way that it cannot be symbolically framed and contained. Both Job and Levi were subject to abjection. Neither recovered; one does not recover from abjection. Not recovery but rather purification resolves abjection, something Job but not Levi was able to do. One might argue that this is because Levi lived in a world in which God was dead, a rationalized and demystified world. One might also argue that this is because Levi underwent an experience in which the absurd disrupted his ability to meaningfully symbolize his experience, almost as though his writings were a symbolic second skin, one that he could never fully embody or inhabit. This would help explain the occasional odd gap between man and narrator.

As Blanchot (1995, 41) pointed out, what disaster requires is body, not meaning: that we be held by the love of another, not by our own frail literary corpus. If the wound is deep enough, not even love is enough, unless perhaps it is that rare, strange perfect love beyond love, such as what Pierre gave to Marie-Louise.

In fact, both of these explanations (i.e., Levi lived in a demystified world, and Levi tried to symbolize what can only be exorcized in bodies in love) are sufficient to explain the occasional odd gap between man and narrator. Yet, there is perhaps a simpler and more awful reason. Levi lived for almost a year surrounded by corpses: sleeping next to corpses, breathing the air filled with the stench and ash of corpses from the crematoria at Auschwitz, talking with men who were virtual walking corpses, some of whom would be corpses by daybreak, men who became corpses within a matter of hours as they were emptied of their bodily fluids by dysentery, corpses lying in their own excrement for hours before Levi or someone like Levi was sent to haul them away to be burned or buried. Is it possible that an experience of such intense abjection, the most intense according to Kristeva (1982, 3) – the abjection of being confronted with corpses, surrounded by corpses, infiltrated by corpses, overwhelmed by corpses, so that one is forever tainted by death – became impossible to purify except through Levi's own death? If so, what could that mean?

Do we think of purification as a primitive ritual, a superstition? What we are really talking about is an experience of dread that runs so deep that it cannot be undone, only covered over: the dread of seeing the corruption of the body, the closeness of the living human body to the dead body, the spirit of animation so tender and fragile. Once one learns that lesson in the particular way Levi learned it, there is no reentering this world again in the same way. It is what the survivor meant when she said, "You're not supposed to see this; it doesn't go with life. It doesn't go with life."

One way Levi could escape the dread of living with death – a dread that was slowly converging with the reality of his imminent physical annihilation as he faced disability and old age – was to become master of his own death.[11] This, of course, remains speculation. What is

---

[11] It is sometimes said that Levi underwent minor surgery in the weeks before his death. This is untrue. He underwent a radical prostatectomy. Levi suffered all the usual side effects, including loss of bladder (and possibly bowel) control, because the operation

not speculation (although the reasons remain far from clear) is the renewed difficulty some survivors experience in old age, after a lifetime of successful adaptation to having lived through hell. The work of Kraft (2002), discussed in the previous chapter, remains the most helpful work on this topic.

When in the midst of a debate with the Berlin historian Ernst Nolte, who doubted the uniqueness of the Holocaust, Levi pointed to the industrial utilization of the body parts, especially the hair and ashes of its victims, as the unique atrocity (Thomson 2002, 523). Surely, Nolte was wrong. The Holocaust is of a different order of magnitude than the crimes of Stalin and Mao, but one wonders about Levi's reasoning. Levi, we recall, lost not a single member of his family to the Holocaust. It was the industrial utilization of the corpses that struck Levi as introducing a unique atrocity into the world. In cold candor, one must reply that this was not central to Hitler's perverse project.

The Holocaust is unique for at least two reasons. First, whereas Stalin and Hitler murdered millions, Hitler and his minions (tens, perhaps hundreds of thousands of them, maybe more) tried to destroy a people, a *genos*, so completely that no one would be left to remember. Second, Hitler and his minions sought not merely to murder but to degrade, humiliate, and torment their victims before finally killing them. Nothing is more troubling yet compelling in Levi's works than the catalogue of unnecessary humiliations – unnecessary even if one's dreadful goal is mass murder. One could interpret the industrial utilization of body parts in this vein, except that this does not seem to be Levi's point. Even if it were, this is only a small (albeit awful) part of the humiliation – humiliation postmortum, so to speak.

did not go smoothly and he had to be returned to the operating room (Angier 2002, 711–12). To the suggestion that he wear incontinence pads, Levi is said to have replied that he couldn't, for then he would be exactly like his mother (Angier 2002, 729). Assuming Levi actually said this, there is no reason to automatically assume that the statement reflects a pathological over-identification with his mother. It is not necessarily neurotic not to want to become frail and incontinent like one's aged mother, and Levi was not necessarily being unrealistic to worry about this possibility at that moment. Context is all. The context in this case is not just psychological but also physical. At the time of his death, Levi was only beginning to recover from serious surgery that left him physically impaired in ways that he must have found humiliating and that may have reminded him of the humanly imposed humiliations of the Lager.

Even as I write this I feel embarrassed, ashamed. First, about whether I should be analyzing Levi's generally sound judgment about the Holocaust in order to say something about the torment suffered by Levi the man. In defense, I argue that while Levi's torment is not as important as what he has to teach us about the Holocaust, Levi's life can teach us about that too. Let us learn as much as we can, while not using what we learn about the teacher to dismiss the lesson. Second, I feel ashamed that the question comes down to whether it is worse to utilize the body parts of murdered millions or to murder a few million more. Is that the level to which we have sunk?

Job, I speculated, may have found the Sirens' call of abjection, the return of the repressed, so attractive that his "restoration," as it is called (42:11–17), was necessary to lure him back to the social world. Levi's situation was different. Although others saw him come fully alive only when talking about his imprisonment and travels home, perhaps this liveliness was superficial. The impress of living with the evidence of his imminent mortality all around him, treated as though he were nothing but a body to be rendered – a walking corpse among thousands of corpses living and dead, an experience taken in through his eyes, nose, ears, and skin – seems to have taken its toll. One wonders (and that is all one can ever do) whether Levi's own death served as that most primitive purification ritual of all, mimesis, by which only death can purify death; Levi's death finally cleansing him of the absurd abjection of surviving a factory whose singular product was the corpse.[12] A corpse that, if all went according to plan, would disappear into smoke and ash, as though the man or woman or child it had once been had never existed.

Spend too much time in this infernal factory, let its smell sink into your bones, and it would not be difficult to be haunted for the rest of your life by the thought that here is the truth of humanity: ashes to ashes, with only a walking corpse in between. Certainly, several of the survivors whose testimony was consulted in the previous chapter – such as Lorna B. (T-1126), who brought burnt chicken bones from her purse to impress on her interviewers what it was like to live infiltrated

---

[12] Girard explores the "essentially mimetic character" of purification ritual in his classic *Violence and the Sacred* (1977, 102–3).

with the memory of the smell of death – confirm the impression that one can be haunted for life by such experiences.

Although Angier's (2002) biography of Levi is helpful, I disagree with her conclusion that:

> For Levi, Auschwitz was an essentially positive experience. It gave him a reason to live . . . to write; it gave him the subject for the contribution he had always known he could make. It was, as he always said, his adventure, his time in Technicolor, his university. (727)

One can understand why Angier would say this – Levi said it himself – however, that is precisely the problem. Levi said it too many times in too many contexts that were, to say the least, out of context. It was, let us say, a half-truth, covering up the other truth: the dread that Auschwitz released, the dread of infinite death, of a world that made no sense and could never be put back together whole again. Levi said this many times as well. Where Angier was correct is in what she shared with Gambetta (1999): the insight that Levi's vulnerability to depression preceded Auschwitz and that his suicide is not traceable directly to Auschwitz. Too many other factors intervened, such as his tortured relationships with his mother and his wife. Because this tormented triangle is covered in the three major English-language biographies of Levi's life (Anissimov 2000; Angier 2002; Thomson 2002), I speak of it no further here.[13]

Auschwitz Spoils Us for the Experience of Job

Auschwitz does not spoil us for the experience of Sisyphus; that experience can be reinterpreted to fit the camps – once, that is, we abandon the quixotic notion that scorn toward one's masters, combined with making the rock your thing, will make anyone but Sisyphus "master of his days" (Camus 1955, 123). Try that at the 186 stone steps of Mauthausen. Mythic suffering turns out to be nothing compared to the real thing. If, however, one understands the experience of Sisyphus as the experience of the sheer will to survive, one day at a time, even when it would be easier to die, then among these survivors one will find survivors of the Holocaust. To this must be added, however, that

---

[13] Anissimov's biography is translated from the French.

among those with exactly the same will to survive are to be counted many of the dead. Not will but luck played the major role. This point Levi always insisted on, and on this point he was correct.[14]

Hannah T. (T-337) made this point when asked by a particularly obtuse and intrusive interviewer how best to commemorate the Holocaust. No monuments, she replied, because survival was luck and so was death. Like one of her mother's brothers who escaped from Poland to Holland, only to be killed by Nazis there. In a sense, she continued, it was all so arbitrary that it becomes impossible to make sense of it. "For me, it was *beshert*" – that is, fate. How, Hanna T. asked, does one commemorate bad-*beshert*?[15] There is, of course, a larger context in which the Holocaust was not bad-fate at all but rather the result of the Germans' planned pleasure in destruction. For Hanna T., it was fate. We read the testimonies of people like Hanna T. not to take their perspective but rather to learn about the world from their experiences.

Auschwitz spoils us not for the experience of Sisyphus; indeed, the experience of Sisyphus was not a human experience, for it was solitary. Even in Auschwitz, many witnesses tell us about friends they made, friends who helped them survive. Hanna T. (T-337) told of her girlfriend, whom she called "her savior." They went through three camps together, and she saved Hannah's life by pulling her through the snow on a sled when Hannah, sick with typhus at liberation, couldn't walk. Without her friend, Hanna T. would have perished in the snow. Some scholars suggest that women inmates relied more on networks of friendship than men (Ofer and Weitzman 1998). That was not my impression, although it is certainly possible that the patterns of friendship differed. Daniel F. (T-153), who was a teenager, told the touching story of holding hands with his new friend as they went everywhere together in Auschwitz-Birkenau, but older inmates also told many stories of cooperating with each other to accomplish the task of survival.

---

[14] In the same interview with Roth quoted previously, Levi responds to Roth's claim that he was a man saved by his skills by saying, "I insist there was no general rule, except entering the camp in good health and knowing German. Barring this, luck dominated." Reflecting a little, Levi qualified this observation, agreeing that thinking and observing were survival factors, but "in my opinion sheer luck predominated" (Levi 2001a, 17).

[15] *Beshert* is a Yiddish word meaning inevitable or predestined. It can be used casually, as it is here, to mean fate or luck.

For Levi, the human warmth gained through cooperation was lifesaving; it is a fragile human thread running through his memoirs of life in the Lager.

In *The Drowned and the Saved*, Levi (1988) told of finding a secret source of water – a slowly dripping pipe – and sharing it with his friend Alberto but not with their equally thirsty friend, Daniele. The memory haunted Levi for years, resurfacing abruptly when Daniele confronted him after the war:

"Why the two of you and not I?" It was the "civilian" moral code surfacing again. . . . I am not able to decide then and I am not able to decide even now, but shame there was and is, concrete, heavy, perennial. (80–1)

Friendship is always exclusive to some degree, but the camps forced on friendship a choiceless choice friends should not have had to make, transforming friendship into "us-ism," the shared version of selfishness (1988, 80).

If the experience of Sisyphus triumphing over the absurd provides only the roughest and, in many ways, misleading approximation of the experience of survivors, the experience of Job toward the end of the Book of Job is not only irrelevant to the experience of Auschwitz. The experience of Job is destroyed by the experience of Auschwitz. Let there be no mistake about my argument. I am not claiming that the experience of transcendence, particularly an experience of transcendence in which nature points beyond itself, ended at Auschwitz. This experience ended for most long before Auschwitz. Some identify the Lisbon earthquake of 1755 as signifying the beginning of the end. More than once, this deadly earthquake has been compared to the Holocaust in terms of its impact on both religion and humanity's confidence in the meaning, the larger significance, of existence. The difference is that today, the Lisbon earthquake seems more explicable – indeed, more tolerable. With lapidary disdain, Adorno (1973, 361) stated, "the earthquake of Lisbon sufficed to cure Voltaire of the theodicy of Leibniz."

Jacques Maritain (1929) located the end of transcendence in nature more than a century earlier, with the philosophy of Descartes, who led modern man to conceive of nature as no more than a set of essences that conform to his reason. In this view, Kant (1965, 118–19) was just playing catch-up. It is with Descartes that "nature was no longer a theophany reflecting God's majesty and power" (Amato 1975, 66; Maritain 1929). My argument does not depend on locating the origins of this centuries-long process; neither is my argument intended to supplant the familiar argument that science has so rationalized the natural world that it is no longer seat of the sublime. About this more familiar argument, I would only remind the reader that for Max Weber, the disenchantment and rationalization of the world owes as much to what he called "workaday [*Alltag*] existence" as it does to science (Weber 1958a, 149). My argument is that Auschwitz adds another dimension. Both the Lisbon earthquake and Cartesian rationalism rendered the natural world more worldly, less divine. Auschwitz renders the social world less rational, more absurd. The result, however, is surprisingly similar, as the natural world becomes more rational by default: *less rationality in the social world = more rationality in the natural world = less chance to experience the natural world as a site of transcendence.* The equation is not automatic, so I explain how it works below.

Surplus Absurdity

Consider the fact the suffering of the inmates at Auschwitz was worse than that of Job. *Hier ist kein warum* takes on a whole new meaning at Auschwitz, for not only does a man suffer for reasons that seem inexplicable, his entire world also is taken from him as he is abducted from his home, robbed of his clothes, shorn of his hair. Job wished he could be sheltered in Sheol until the Lord's wrath was past. Levi was removed to the depths of hell. Levi described "the typical prisoner" in Job-like terms, "hungry, weakened, covered with sores, especially on the feet" (1988, 160). However, for Levi, unlike Job, there were no friends to offer the infuriating but nonetheless familiar explanations of Deuteronomic theology, explanations with which Job can argue and so maintain his dignity. There is no cynical wife to recommend that he "curse God and die," spousal advice that although hardly a comfort, at least had the advantage of being familiar. Job lived in a mythic world – a world of types – and in this world, he has a place until the end, when God makes His appearance. Not that God is a great comfort either, for God does not explain Himself in terms that Job had expected. Nevertheless, the fact that the world has a *warum*, even if Job will never understand it, turns out to be a remarkable comfort to Job, for that is the message of the Lord of the whirlwind.

What we must consider is whether it is possible to read the Book of Job in the same way after Auschwitz – not simply because God seems to have abandoned His Chosen People, for if God's will is as inscrutable as the Book of Job suggests, that is not for us to know. Rather, because Auschwitz seems to have made it even more difficult to believe that natural beauty, the experience of the transcendent and sublime, tells us anything about our moral situation on this planet. Natural beauty and the sublime remain, but they are immanent categories, pointing to nothing beyond themselves; for if they did, they could not avoid pointing right past (or, rather, through) Auschwitz. In other words, Auschwitz marks a turning point in which the human absurd, what I call "surplus absurdity," exceeds natural absurdity.[16] The result is to rationalize the natural world while transforming the social world into the site of the absurd.

Recall Camus's (1955, 28) definition of the absurd: "The absurd is born of this confrontation between the human need and the unreasonable silence of the world." We should not take the term "unreasonable silence of the world" as a condemnation, any more than it is reasonable condemnation to call a rock stupid because it does not speak. The world just is and because it just is, it would make no sense to call the world absurd.

Nor is human life absurd. Humans make plans, dream dreams, dominate others, fall in love, and die. That's not absurd either but merely human. Absurd is the conjunction – or better, disjunction – between the world and humanity. Humans long for the world to participate in some way in their hopes and dreams, to share in their lives, to acknowledge their existence. It is the incommensurability between the world's mere being and humanity's terrible longing for a reply that generates the experience of absurdity. Camus called it *nostalgia* (*nostalgie*), which is a perfectly good word as long as we understand that one can experience nostalgia – perhaps the strongest and most persistent nostalgia – for that which one never had (1955, 28).

---

[16] There might be more than one turning point in the history of the relationship between natural and surplus absurdity.

Immediately after characterizing the naturalism of absurdity in Franz Kafka, Camus went on to make a statement that is revealing and concealing in equal measure: "There is in the human condition (and this is a commonplace of all literatures) a basic absurdity as well as an implacable nobility. The two coincide, as is natural" (Camus 1955, 127). Yes, they coincide, they cannot be completely distinguished, but they are not the same, and Camus made insufficient effort to disentangle them. I say this even as Camus in a footnote stated clearly that Kafka's works are "quite legitimately" interpreted as social criticism, not merely as expressions of "supernatural anxiety," what Kierkegaard called *angst*. "It is probable, moreover, that there is no need to choose. Both interpretations are good. In absurd terms, as we have seen, revolt against men is also directed against God: great revolutions are always metaphysical" (Camus 1955, 127).

Whereas one does not need to choose for metaphysical purposes, one needs to choose for practical, even political, purposes – although not the political purposes Conor Cruise O'Brien (1970) had in mind when he argued that one reason the rats will return to infest Oran, site of *The Plague* (1972), is that they will come "from the quarter in which the narrator had refused to look; from the houses which the good Dr. Rieux never visited.... The source of the plague is what we pretend is not there" (70). O'Brien, of course, is referring to the Arab quarter, or should one say three quarters, of Oran, in Algeria, about whose fate Camus was notoriously ambiguous.

Much earlier, Roland Barthes argued that Camus's novel about the plague was misleading because one cannot adequately compare the moral dilemmas facing the Resistance with those of men and women fighting microbes. This is a long and familiar line of criticism, and Camus's answer is in a letter to Barthes written in 1955 (Camus 1968, 338–41). My argument, I believe, is more than a generalization of this line of criticism.

Marcuse wrote of surplus repression, by which he meant that amount of psychological repression necessary to maintain the dominance hierarchy of a competitive capitalistic system, as compared to the lesser amount of repression necessary to maintain civilization itself, so that society does not devolve into a group of sex maniacs, as he once put it (Marcuse 1966, 37).

I propose that we think about absurdity in an analogous fashion. A significant amount of absurdity is inherent in the human condition, given the longings of human beings, the silence of nature, and the way in which humanity and nature are interwoven. However, much absurdity is "surplus," serving the interests of hierarchy, domination, and confusion, and thereby the exploitation of the weak by the strong – even if the strong are as mystified by absurdity as the weak. Better to be mystified while eating a good meal in a nice restaurant and then going home to sleep in a warm bed than to be bewildered while hungry, cold, and homeless. One imagines, for example, that the bubonic plague was worse in some crowded quarters of Oran, where the garbage was infrequently collected and the rats more numerous, as they are in ghettos almost everywhere.

There is another reason to posit a poetic parallel (for that is what we are discussing) between Marcuse's surplus repression and surplus absurdity. Marcuse's concept intentionally confused the psychological concept of repression developed by Freud – which assumed that repression is strictly an intrapsychic developmental process – with social repression, the consequence of capitalism and instrumental reason. Similarly, there is something intentionally confusing about surplus absurdity, as though one could subtract from the absurdity that afflicts all humans the portion that the strong inflict on the weak. However absurdity works, it is not as proportional or as logical as that.

True enough, but the point remains. If we see no difference between the absurdity of a silent nature that kills without explanation and a silent judicial system that does the same, or a capricious plague and a capricious economic system that we defend in nature-like terms such as "the forces of the market," then we have turned the absurd into our god, worshiping at the altar of a new antihumanism as though it were an idol. Camus never made this mistake, at least not in practice. As with Marcuse's concept of surplus repression, "surplus absurdity" stands not so much as a utopian goal as a measure of social domination. With such rational mileposts, hope is unnecessary – at least, as long as hope is conceived as nostalgia for a lost unity between humanity and nature.

However, humans are not so rational. Like it or not (and there is no reason not to fall in love with the idea), humans will always long for a lost unity, an Eden before The Fall. And why not? Are we not remembering traces in our lives – as infants, lovers, and accomplices of nature – when for a moment the *promesse de bonhure* was fulfilled? As Levi said shortly after being liberated from Auschwitz:

We were contented because that day (we did not know about the next, but what happens tomorrow is not always important) we could do things we had not done for too long: drink water from a well, stretch out in the sun in the middle of tall robust grass, smell the summer air... go into the woods in search of strawberries and mushrooms, smoke a cigarette looking at the high sky swept clean by the wind. (Levi 1995, 135)

One wonders whether Levi had many moments like this in the years following his liberation from Auschwitz.

"A nice story about Levi," the critical reader might reply, "but stick to the point." No matter how you slice it, absurdity is not a qualitative category, much less a quantitative one. The trouble is, Camus didn't say that; he said the opposite. If life is absurd, then what counts is "not the best living but the most living" (Camus 1955, 60–1). Camus went on to explain that by the "most living," he meant living for something truly worth the trouble of living, and that along the way one should judge oneself occasionally (1955, 64–5). It seems as though there is a qualitative moment built into the very heart of the concept of the absurd.

Is the world more absurd if the wealthy citizens of Oran force the poor into rat-infested ghettos so that the rich can remain healthy and unmolested in their airy villas outside of town? (This scenario is my own; for Camus, enclosure and entrapment haunt the lives of all who live in Oran.) The world is rendered less just, less fair, but no more or no less absurd, for absurdity is an attribute of the human condition *tout court*. Perhaps not. If we understand absurdity as the intersection of humanity and nature, having strictly the quality of a relationship between humanity and nature, then altering the terms by which one of the partners encounters the other may indeed alter the way in which absurdity is experienced by that partner capable of experiencing absurdity.

Consider a fascinating remark by Jean Tarrou, a faintly mysterious character in *The Plague*, about what is natural:

What's natural is the microbe. All the rest – health, integrity, purity (if you like) – is a product of the human will, of a vigilance that must never falter. The good man... is the man who has the fewest lapses of attention. (Camus 1972, 235–6)

Here, it seems fair to set the absurdity of nature, in the form of the plague, against the human will, which cries out against the absurd. If the human will (admittedly a reification, so we must talk about individual wills and the collective organization of society) cries out one way as it encounters nature, we will experience absurdity differently than if it cries out in another way. Will the result actually be less absurdity if my will acts in concert with other wills, rather than colluding with some wills to evade the plague at the expense of others? The answer to this question is unimportant. Absurdity, as Camus said in his introduction to *The Myth of Sisyphus*, is a sensitivity, not a philosophy (1955, 2). If it is a sensitivity, then we have to be especially sensitive to the way in which absurdity may be socially mobilized.

Do the witnesses interviewed in Chapter 3 suffer from surplus absurdity? Yes, for what else is doubling as the loss of value but a response to an absurd world, a world in which every value expressive of life is transformed into a value expressive of death, a world in which there is no *warum*? Not because nature is silent and therefore austere and awesome but rather because men and women have chosen to make the human world a dark mirror of nature, in which the face that could recognize another human turns away. In this world of choiceless choice, doubling is a response to the loss of value that is tantamount to the loss of meaning. When humans choose to make the social world as unresponsive as – and, more wantonly, destructive than – the natural, the result is surplus absurdity. Doubling is how humans survive such a world.

Levi is also a witness and, as I have suggested, perhaps he did not double enough, imagining that he could confront Auschwitz in his books and so liberate himself. Witnesses tell us it isn't so. That too is a lesson of the testimonies. Testimony is many things, but it does not heal. A character in a recent novel by Philip Roth (an author who not only interviewed Levi but also became his friend late in Levi's life) expressed it more simply when he said:

When Primo Levi killed himself everyone said it was because of his having been an inmate at Auschwitz. I thought it was because of his *writing* about Auschwitz, the labor of the last book, contemplating that horror with all that clarity. Getting up every morning to write that book would have killed anyone. (2007, 151)

The Holocaust Is Not Sublime

To the degree that we experience the human encounter with nature as absurd, nature remains mysterious, awesome, and infuriating in its seeming willful disregard for human happiness. Nature's continued status as site of the sublime depends (and perhaps this is a paradox) on its absurdity – that is, its silent obscurity.[17] Nature may become less absurd in two ways. With the first we are familiar, in which science and technology help us better understand nature and so feel less the hunted, more the hunter, even if the final hunt will always be nature's trophy.

The other way nature becomes less absurd is when the social world becomes more absurd. When *hier gibt es kein warum* applies more readily to human creations such as bureaucracies of humiliation and death than it does even to the plague (for, against the former, as Levi argued, virtually no social organization was possible), then nature itself loses its nimbus because it loses the quality of the absurd that contributes to that aura: the silent, unresponsive givenness that simply is, beyond good and evil. Nature remains these things but the experience is overwhelmed, denatured, by the human horror of Auschwitz and all it represents. Culture, second-nature, becomes the realm of the absurd as the natural order – once the realm of silent beauty and terror – becomes the only order on which we can depend. In other words, nature becomes rational in comparison to (and perhaps as defense against) the caprice of the social. Whatever virtues such a nature possesses, it can no longer play host to the sublime.

The consequence, as Weber (1958c) pointed out, is the ironic one of isolating transcendent experience within the specialized province of the worship of the divine:

Culture's every step forward seems condemned to lead to an ever more devastating senselessness. . . . The need for "salvation" responds to this devaluation by becoming more other-worldly, more alienated from all structured forms of life, and, in exact parallel, by confining itself to the specific religious essence. This reaction is the stronger the more systematic the thinking about the "meaning" of the universe becomes, the more the external organization of the world is rationalized, and the more the conscious experience of the world's irrational content is sublimated. (357)

---

[17] In relationship to humanity and its needs, which is Camus's (1955, 28) definition of the absurd.

The sublime, according to Kant (1987, sec. 23–27), is the transgression of human categories by an overwhelming experience that
exceeds our powers of imagination. Our imagination, which we naïvely
assumed to be limitless, is suddenly confronted by that which it cannot
encompass, such as the vast and limitless power of God and His creation. This suggested to Lang (2000, 56–7) that because the sublime
rests on an experience of transgression, in which experience overwhelms the imagination, the Holocaust itself might represent a per-
version of the sublime. "Transgression downward," Lang (57) called
it, in which "radical evil," as Kant referred to it elsewhere, surpasses
the imagination for evil.[18]

Whether or not the Holocaust is unimaginable, it is certainly difficult to represent, so much so that its depiction involves more blurring
of genres than that of almost any other historical event (Lang 2000,
35). Consider, for example, Daniel Goldhagen's (1996) account of
the role played by a particularly widespread and virulent strain of
anti-Semitism, almost unique to Germany, in the destruction of the
Jews. Suddenly, almost out of nowhere (or so it seems), Goldhagen is
imagining a postcoital dialogue between concentration camp guards:

The Germans made love in barracks next to enormous privation and incessant
cruelty. What did they talk about when their heads rested on their pillows,
when they were smoking their cigarettes in those relaxing moments after
their physical needs had been met? Did one relate to another accounts of a
particularly amusing beating that she or he had administered or observed,
of the rush of power that engulfed her when the righteous adrenaline of
Jew-beating caused her body to pulse with energy? (339)

---

[18] Kant's (1960, 30–2) concept of radical evil did not refer to the extremity of the
act, as Lang, among so many others, seemed to assume. Kant's concept referred to
a defect (*malum defectus*) of the will, which transforms morality into the servant of
desire, so that we can do what we will with a good conscience. Radical evil is thus
applicable to a much wider range of acts than those we might ordinarily call evil,
referring as it does to the self-deceit behind the act. Nevertheless, Lang's use of the
term, referring both to the imagination-shattering intensity and magnitude of the
act, is now the accepted one, and I follow Lang's lead.

In an earlier work, Arendt refers to radical evil as the way in which individuals are
rendered superfluous by terror, becoming mere masses. Arendt made explicit the
distinction between her use of the term and Kant's (1973, ix, 443, 458–9). Later,
after covering the trial of Adolf Eichmann for *The New Yorker* magazine, Arendt would
come to give up her belief in radical evil, saying, "it is indeed my opinion now that
evil is never 'radical,' that it is only extreme." The passage is from an "acrimonious
exchange" between Arendt and Gershom Scholem (Elshtain 1995, 76). What Arendt
was trying to say is that evil is not radical because it has no depth; that is its banality.

What is it about the Holocaust that leads even the sober historian to fantasize about the sexual lives of concentration camp guards?

Goldhagen's hatred is certainly part of the answer. Presuming that these fictional guards were not ranking officers (and perhaps even if they were), they probably went on to live normal lives in postwar Germany, raising children, never thinking, never having to think, about what went on in the other "barracks" next door. Certainly, tens of thousands of real guards did. Incomprehension is another part of the answer: that humans could take such pleasure in evil. For that is the issue that Goldhagen was raising, a key reason his book was so successful among the public, even as it failed to convince many scholars. Germans tormented, degraded, and killed Jews because they wanted to, because they liked to do it, because it made them feel powerful and good and clean and righteous to do so. That is the distasteful secret behind the vast commercial success of *Hitler's Willing Executioners*: more than a half-million books sold in the Americas and Europe. Yet, the large number of books sold suggests that this secret was hardly a secret at all.

What is so difficult to imagine is what we already know. Knowledge as disaster, Blanchot called it. The problem isn't learning something new; the problem is accepting what we know about ourselves and humanity: something terribly simple and simply terrible. Under certain circumstances, most people (not everyone), when given unlimited power over others who have already been degraded, devalued, and dehumanized, will use this power to degrade, dehumanize, and ultimately destroy these others. Furthermore, there is no larger metaphysical reason despite recent attempts to transform the language of the Other into an explanation: People don't like to hurt the Other. They like to hurt particular other people in particular circumstances, especially when they are invited to do so. This involves two steps: first, permission by those in authority; and, second, the degradation of the victims. The fact that the victims are ruined by those who will then use their degradation as an excuse to humiliate and destroy them makes no difference. The only logic at work here is psycho-logic.[19]

---

[19] My argument diverges from Goldhagen (1996), arguing but certainly not proving that pleasure in destruction, not an ideology he called "eliminationist anti-Semitism," played the major role. However, my argument is not in principle incompatible with Goldhagen's. An ideology of vicious anti-Semitism may be seen as providing the

To a person of ordinary imagination, historical literacy, and psychological insight, the Holocaust is quite imaginable. This statement applies even to that most terrible act, to which Heinrich Himmler and his tens of thousands of followers came shockingly close, "that this people should disappear from the earth" (Lang 2000, 3).

Saul Friedlander (1993, 109–11) referred to the *Rausch*, the intoxication of destruction, which seems to have seized Himmler and other Nazi leaders as the goal of destroying an entire people came within their grasp. Is this unimaginable? Why should it be? Pleasure in destruction, in destroying the innocent and good because it is innocent and good, has a long history. Is this not what Milton's Satan meant when he said simply, "Evil be thou my Good"? (*Paradise Lost* IV, 105–10). When William Blake said that Satan gets all the best lines in *Paradise Lost*, he was not kidding. Satan is often an attractive figure, just as evil may be attractive, which should be cause for deep concern. Although it was pears and not people that he destroyed, the fact that he destroyed them out of the sheer pleasure in destruction bothered Augustine for years (*Confessions* II.III.9)[20] – as well it should have.

Hope, enlightenment, faith in reason, progress, belief in a particular human vision of God (a hubristic vision Job learns, as though God should conform to our vision of Him): All this and more is transgressed by the Holocaust. However, to claim that the destruction of these human ideals is the inversion of the sublime, reality shattering the bounds of the imagination for evil, says more about the narrowness of our imagination than anything else; or, rather, about the blinders we put on our self-knowledge, individually and collectively – that is, as historians of our species.

However, what we know and imagine now about evil is vastly different than what we knew or could imagine in 1930, is it not? Of course, or there would be nothing new to learn, no history from which to learn. My claim is simply that barbarism, the lust to destroy, and pleasure in mass murder did not begin or end then. To be sure, the Holocaust did

opportunity, when institutionalized, to exercise pleasure in cruelty and dominion one would otherwise be unable to express. Chapter 5 discusses the institutionalization of cruelty and dominion in more detail.

[20] Eventually, Augustine concluded that he destroyed the pears for other reasons, in order to belong to the group of pear thieves. I'm not sure he even convinced himself (*Confessions*, II.viii.16).

bring something new to our knowledge of evil: that it is subject to an absurd rationalization, captured far better by Raul Hilberg's (1985) account of the German railways (*Reichsbahn*) schedule of fares to bring passengers to the concentration camps than any sado-sexual fantasy Goldhagen could imagine:

The basic charge was the third-class fare: 4 pfennig per track kilometer. Children under 10 were transported for half this amount; those under four went free.... For the deportees one-way fare was payable; for the guards a round-trip ticket had to be purchased. (411)

With this rationalization of destruction, the Holocaust did bring something new into the world, similar to the banality of evil that Arendt (1965) wrote of, but which I have suggested comes closer to the absurdity of evil. The absurdity of evil is akin to the world of Kafka, in which the rationality of everyday life goes on in heightened form even as the goals it serves become more obscure, evil, and obscene. Perhaps the obscurity of the goals, the mark of absurdity, is itself a defense against knowledge of the evil that seemingly rational men and women are pursuing, but about this I am not sure. I am sure that this is no new idea but rather a version of the *Dialectic of Enlightenment* of Horkheimer and Adorno (2002), in which extreme rationalization is bound to the return of ever more mythic goals of *blut und boden* – purity and human sacrifice.

While the Holocaust brought something new to the world, there was nothing sublime (not even the inverse of the sublime) about it. The Holocaust did not shatter the imagination, only mocked it, combining evil and rationality in ways too humanly comprehensible to register as transgression, too absurd to understand in a satisfactory manner. When asked for an explanation of the Holocaust, generally we want more: that it makes sense, which often means that the end was present in the beginning if only we could have seen it. This seems to be what Levi meant when he concluded from the impossibility of a complete explanation that no explanation is possible (Levi 2001b, 232). One consequence is that we are led further and further from the one explanation that really works in these matters – an explanation that is not really an explanation at all but rather a re-description of what happened in terms of the simplest of human motives. For various simple and complex reasons that we need not and generally do not understand, people do what they want to do. Germans and others tormented and killed Jews, gypsies, homosexuals, and others because they wanted to, because it gave them pleasure to do so. Is this not transgression enough?

The Holocaust is not a universal sign or metaphor but rather an act of destruction initiated by one exclusionary group against another group, based on the first group's conception of its identity in terms of its will and power to deny not just identity but also existence to another group.[21] To see the Holocaust as the inversion of the sublime, or some such, is to confuse surplus absurdity with natural absurdity. The Holocaust is absurd because some people have rendered the human world so morally incomprehensible that it becomes almost impossible to see one's way out. We should not underestimate the destructive power of the absurd on the human psyche. Maritain's future wife, Raïssa, wrote in 1902 that she and Jacques had been unhappily strolling about in the *Jardin des Plantes*. None of their professors at the Sorbonne seemed to have anything to say that was relevant to their lives. Yet, she said, "I would have accepted a sad life, but not one that was absurd." She and Jacques made what was in effect a suicide pact. If they could not find some meaning in life before their youth was spent, "we wanted to die by a free act if it were impossible to live according to the truth" (Maritain 1961, 69). Fortunately, they soon encountered the *Lebensphilosophie* of Henri Bergson.

Equally fortunate are we that the antidote to absurdity is not necessarily philosophy at all. Levi told us about the joy with which he experienced nature for the first time since being liberated from Auschwitz:

I had been walking for hours in the marvelous morning air, drawing it into my battered lungs like medicine.... I felt an imperious need to take possession of my body again, to re-establish a contact, by now broken for almost two years, with trees and grass, with the heavy brown soil. (Levi 1995, 106; see also 135)

Sometimes the reality of a normal, human everyday life is enough. To see the Holocaust as a transgression on the order of the sublime is to reify its power to occlude all that lies beyond it, granting Auschwitz a transcendent status that it does not deserve. Even Levi did not escape this confusion when he seized on the ghetto as a metaphor for the

---

[21] This represents a strengthening of Lang's conclusion (2000, 132).

human condition. "We are all in the ghetto, that the ghetto is walled in, that outside the ghetto reign the lords of death, and that close by the train is waiting" (1988, 69). In expressing it in this way, Levi rendered surplus absurdity akin to natural absurdity, even the transcendent. His was a grave mistake because it makes ordinary social and political analysis impossible. Levi rarely succumbed to the temptations of transcendent abstraction; among those who write on the Holocaust, it is not uncommon.

The Concentration Camp Is Not an Idea

Arendt's *The Origins of Totalitarianism* (1973) should be helpful in conducting this ordinary social and political analysis, for Arendt made the concentration camps central to the totalitarian ideal, as she called it. However, this is really the problem. In the end, the concentration camps represented an idea for Arendt, the culmination of the totalitarian idea, which is itself an idea – that of pure uncontaminated logic, "ice-cold reasoning," in which consequences flow with a logic all their own, bereft of human intervention and feeling.[22]

To be sure, Arendt understood that the camps existed not merely to kill but also to degrade and dehumanize their victims (1973, 438). Arendt also understood that the horror of the camps can never be fully communicated or reported, for there are no parallels to life in the concentration camps. "It can never be fully reported for the very reason that the survivor returns to the world of the living, which makes it impossible to believe fully in his own past experience" (1973, 444).

Certainly, many of the witnesses said just this. Yet, Arendt took her own insight too far, arguing that only those who have not experienced the terror firsthand "can afford to keep thinking about the horrors" (444). Only those who have not experienced the horror firsthand can write about the horror with perspective.

Arendt was wrong. Primo Levi proved that she was wrong. Améry proved that she was wrong. Delbo proved that she was wrong, even if all paid a terrible price. Almost all of the witnesses prove that she

---

[22] I am not concerned with the academic issue of whether Arendt was correct that totalitarianism is a new phenomenon. The issue is adequately discussed by John Stanley (1987), among others. Not the uniqueness of totalitarianism, but Arendt's use of the concept to understand the concentration camps is my concern.

was wrong, including Eva L., the witness who asked, "How can they believe if I can't believe?" Eva L. went on to talk simply but eloquently for more than an hour about the hardships she continues to endure, including her longing for her first family while in the midst of her second.

Why would Arendt imagine that those who stood too close to the horror would be so transfixed by it that they could not think, write, or talk convincingly about it? Part of the answer has to do with Arendt's theory of rhetoric, if that is what it is. "The more authentic they are," said Arendt, the more accounts of suffering in the camps transform men into "uncomplaining animals" being led to the slaughter. Such accounts can never inspire the "passions of outrage and sympathy which inspire men to seek justice" (439). In other words, we best not look or listen too closely lest we learn a truth about suffering that inspires not action but stunned paralysis. I do not believe this is true, but it is worth remembering that *Origins of Totalitarianism* was originally published in 1950 and completed even earlier. Many survivors state that on their liberation and for many years after, no one wanted to hear their story. Some survivors waited years to tell theirs. Time changes everything (even if it heals nothing), particularly that time marked in generations and our ability to hear the horror changes with it.

In Arendt's case, there appears to be another reason she preferred to keep her theoretical distance. For Arendt, the concentration camp was itself an idea. The concentration camp was the testing ground that proved totalitarianism (1973, 437). The concentration camp exemplified the key idea of totalitarianism – that terror makes the many into one "by pressing men against each other," leaving no space among them (464). Not only was this literally true of the concentration camps – just look at the photographs of the "barracks" taken shortly after liberation: three and four men or women sleeping together in a single bunk, the bunks stacked floor to ceiling. It was true in an equally profound and abstract sense, in which each person was reduced to a being driven by primordial fear. Terror erases plurality among men and women, that key category of Arendt's, eliminating difference and distinction. Under terror, we are all the same under the skin for we are all, in a sense, nothing but our skin, this incredibly vulnerable covering. What's inside no longer matters, no longer exists.

The result is a profound loneliness, as men and women are no longer able to talk even to themselves. For no "two-in-one" remains, a category Arendt introduced here and developed only later, to refer to a man who has not yet lost "trust in himself as the partner of his thought" (476). It is not difficult to see the two-in-one as an act of ordinary doubling. The doubling we all do every day of our lives – unless we are unfortunate enough to be overwhelmed by extreme trauma, in which case we lose our ability to talk to ourselves, becoming overwhelmed by images of horror.

Arendt was not simply mistaken. In some respects, her insight into terror was profound. Only now we see that her insight into the concentration camp stemmed from her most abstract ideas about the modern world: that the concentration camp is itself a product of mass society, in which men and women become superfluous and lonely, isolated and uprooted in private as well as in public life. "The totalitarian attempt to make men superfluous reflects the experience of modern masses of their superfluity on an overcrowded earth" (1973, 457). Arendt continued:

Loneliness, the common ground for terror, the essence of totalitarian government, and . . . the preparation of its executioners and victims, is closely connected with uprootedness and superfluousness which have been the curse of modern masses since the beginning of the industrial revolution and have become acute with the rise of imperialism at the end of the last century and the break-down of political institutions and social traditions in our own time. (1973, 475)

About Arendt's theoretical connection between the concentration camp and mass society, I do not judge except to point out that it is not mine. My argument about surplus absurdity does not depend on an elaborate and particular social theory. Indeed, surplus absurdity is not a social theory as much as it is an empirical observation: that as the social world becomes more irrational, even (or especially) in its rationality – an ironic category captured by Kafka and the Frankfurt School – the natural world becomes ever more rational by default. The result is that the natural world loses any possibility it once had as a source of spiritual inspiration and transcendence, whereas the social world becomes more obscure and reified than it need be.

In any case, the concentration camp is not primarily an idea, the point Adorno (1967, 34) was trying to make with his notorious remark about it being barbaric to write poetry after Auschwitz. To make the concentration camp an idea, even a good one, is to mirror just a little too closely the ideology Arendt criticized. Not the ideology of totalitarianism but rather ideology itself, which – as Arendt (1973, 469) pointed out – is never interested in the present and prides itself on its ignorance of the particular in favor of the general and universal.

5

Conclusion: Beyond the Silence of Job

Man, being a brave animal and one accustomed to pain, does not necessarily flee suffering. Often enough, he seeks it out, provided he can grasp a meaning for it. Being a sickly animal, suffering generally finds humanity out, whether or not humanity goes looking for it. Man's problem is not and never was that he suffers, "but that there was no answer to the crying question, '*Why* do I suffer?'" (Nietzsche 1968a, 598 [iii, 28]) – at least, not since the death of God who, according to Nietzsche, has been moribund for some time (Nietzsche 1974, 180 [iii, 125]).

The Book of Job reveals that the issue is not quite so straightforward: Not only does Job not know why he suffers, but his odyssey ends when he learns from God that he is never going to find out. Job also learns that there is an order in the universe that culminates in a sublime beauty in which he – and we – may participate. This frames his suffering in an experience of transcendence, soothing his sorrow – or, rather, it soothes the suffering reader, who presumably will not be restored as Job was.

Auschwitz does not destroy the experience of the sublime. Auschwitz, however, contributes more than its share to the transformation of the human world into the site of absurdity, in which to expect an answer (even sixty years later) to the question "*Warum?*" is even more absurd than to expect the universe to answer the question, "Why was I born if it wasn't forever?"[1]

---

[1] The quotation is from Eugène Ionesco's play, *Exit the King* (1962). King Berenger's next line is: "Damn my parents!"

The result is a long train of events, seeming to culminate in Auschwitz – but, in reality, only pausing there – in which the social world becomes increasingly more absurd than the natural, with the consequent impoverishment of both worlds. The social world becomes a site of reification, whereas the natural world loses its ability to evoke our experience of the sublime[2] – or, rather, the sublime can no longer point beyond itself, as it did for Job. The sublime is no longer a sign but an emptiness. The sublime explodes human categories, while leaving no trace of the transcendent behind.

Elijah stands on the mountain, waiting for the word of the Lord. First came a wind, rending the mountains, but the Lord was not in the wind. Then came an earthquake, but the Lord was not in the shattering rocks, nor in the fire that followed. Only then came a still small voice (*dmamah daq qowl*), as though God were whispering in the silence that followed the awesome expressions of nature's power (1 Kings 11–12) – as though nature's majesty served only to heighten by contrast the stillness that follows. What happens when we can no longer hear the silence? What happens when not only God's voice but also the Sirens' call is stilled, so that the symbolic is no longer moved by the semiotic?

Is it heresy to equate God's voice with the Sirens' call? Perhaps to some; to others, both represent our unconscious resonance with the deepest sources of meaning, wholeness, and fulfillment. Kristeva called it the *chora*. For Plato, in *The Timaeus*, the *chora* is:

> ...the mother and receptacle of all created and visible and in any way sensible things...an invisible and formless being which receives all things and in some mysterious way partakes of the intelligible and most incomprehensible. (51a–b)

It is no wonder that Plato is carrying *The Timaeus* as he walks with Aristotle while pointing to the heavens in Raphael's "The School of Athens." The *chora* sounds like an abstract, monotheistic God or, at least, the mother of God.

---

[2] *Reification* is a term with a long and checkered history, beginning with Georg Lukács. I understand the term roughly as Axel Honneth does in *Reification: A New Look at an Old Idea* (2008). Reification is in effect whenever people treat each other (or themselves) as things – that is, as objects lacking rich inner worlds.

The framework within which human evil acted at Auschwitz was described by Weber (1958b, 181), who died in the interwar years, as the "iron cage of rationalization." The same administration that administers the bureaucracy of everyday life administered the bureaucracy of death over which men like Eichmann, rightly called a *Schreibtischmörder* (desk murderer), presided. Levi understood that Kafka's *The Trial* must be combined with Weber's iron cage to truly capture the absurdity at the heart of contemporary experience.

In 1982, Levi translated *The Trial* into Italian, remarking that Kafka inspired in him a "repulsion that is clearly of a psychoanalytic nature" (Levi 2001b, 101). Levi said he felt "contaminated" by Joseph K., Kafka's protagonist, perhaps because Levi saw a similarity between his life and Kafka's own. What Levi pointed to was the similarity in narrative structure between *The Trial* and *Survival in Auschwitz*, both books narrating senseless events in the tone of a dispassionate courtroom testimonial (Thomson 2002, 434). In fact, the stylistic similarities between Kafka and Levi are superficial, even antithetical: Levi used his limpid, lapidary style to create the illusion of clarity and understanding; Kafka used his to give everyday events the nimbus of unreality and horror.[3] Nevertheless, both were trapped in this absurd world, and from this position there is more to learn than one might think. How might humans live decently and humanely in a world from which there is no escape, no transcendence, in which the only nimbus is the aura of horror?

Allow me to repeat myself so that there is no mistake about my argument. I am not claiming that the experience of transcendence, particularly as expressed in an experience of the sublimity of nature, ended at Auschwitz. This experience ended for many long before Auschwitz; for some, it still exists. My claim is that with Auschwitz, the natural world becomes by default more rational, less absurd than the social because the social world became insane. This is the meaning of surplus absurdity. In such a world, it becomes ever more difficult to

---

[3] About Kafka, Levi said he is "like a huge machine advancing on you, like a prophet who tells you the day of your death." Angier interpreted this "huge machine" as depression but was rightly skeptical of Levi's claim, in an interview with Germaine Greer, that his depression, the worst since the 1960s, was entirely due to translating Kafka. Angier went on to suggest other sources (Angier 2002, 631).

escape Weber's iron cage via an experience of the sublime, which at best takes on the quality of a day pass from prison. The prison of rationalization of everyday life may be compensated for, as Weber (1958c, 357) suggested, by moments of transcendence limited to the specialized realms of religion and, one should add, art. Once the rationality of everyday [*Alltag*] life is itself thoroughly threatened by the absurd, there is no standpoint from which to transcend and no place to which to transcend. Whereas spatial metaphor as an explication of transcendence may seem heavy-handed, about topics such as transcendence there is only metaphor or silence. More subtle metaphors are not necessarily less misleading.

Attention as Worship in an Absurd World

Is there an alternative to the experience of the sublime that might at least allow us to see the light that shines between the prison bars? In other words, is there an alternative path to transcendence, one compatible with life in the iron cage – even an iron cage located in an absurd world? Paying attention is an alternative for living within and amid absurdity, an alternative whose possibilities are only hinted at by Camus's Tarrou when he states that "the good man . . . is the man who has the fewest lapses of attention" (1972, 236). For Tarrou, we pay attention to ourselves so that we do not carelessly infect others. He is talking about the plague, but there are many ways to infect others: for example, with careless remarks or by a careless exercise of one's social and political position – above all, by not paying attention to particular others, and so treating them as generic humans – that is, human objects.

Camus used the term *attention* with no apparent reference to his admired contemporary, Simone Weil, who elaborated the concept. Camus published eight of Weil's works, finding in them and Weil both a welcome alternative to nihilism and a troubling idealization of suffering[4] (Todd 1997, 290–1; Gray 2001, 218). (Shortly before leaving to accept the Nobel Prize, Camus spent an hour at Weil's house in France.) For Weil, *attention* means to suspend thinking, leaving

---

[4] Camus edited a book series, *Espoir* [Hope], launched in 1946, for the publishing house Gallimard. It eventually grew to twenty-four works (Todd 1997, 290–1).

one's mind detached, empty, ready to be entered by the other. *Attention* means not always trying to know, not categorizing but waiting, as though the other could participate in forming the idea we have of it. *Attention* is the opposite of a thought that has seized on some idea too hastily and thinks it knows (Weil 1977c). Weil's view was similar in some respects to what Adorno (1973) called *negative dialectics*, or mimesis.

More fruitful for our purposes is how the term *attention* was adapted and adopted by Iris Murdoch, Oxford don and novelist, who was deeply influenced by Weil, more so than by any other woman (Conradi 2001, 260): "The enemies of art and of morals, that is, the enemies of love, are the same: social convention and neurosis," wrote Murdoch. With the term *neurosis*, Murdoch referred to fantasies that "inflate the importance of the self and obscure the reality of others." Convention refers to the tendency of the individual to become "sunk in a social whole which we allow uncritically to determine our reactions, or because we see each other exclusively as so determined" (Murdoch 1999, 216).

Both obscure our vision of the particular other, what Murdoch (1970) called *attention*, a term she drew from Weil "to express the idea of a just and loving gaze directed upon an individual reality" (30). "Love is the perception of individuals. Love is the extremely difficult realisation that something other than oneself is real" (Murdoch 1999, 215). The goal is to see the other person justly, honestly, and compassionately. Doing so means moving away from universality and principles and toward increasing depth, privacy, and particularity. "The central concept of morality," said Murdoch, "is 'the individual' thought of as knowable by love" (1970, 30). That's attention.

Was Murdoch just borrowing a term from Weil or was she borrowing a way of thinking? For Weil, attention was preparation for an encounter with God. For Murdoch, attention was the way we open ourselves to the experiences of other humans. However, perhaps these are not so different after all. In the legend of the Holy Grail, the vessel belongs to the seeker who first asks its guardian, a king paralyzed by a painful wound, "What are you going through?" (Weil 1977c, 51). That is paying attention. Attention turns us from ourselves, opening us to the experiences of other people.

Attention stems from a religious tradition in which one opens oneself to God. However, as portrayed by Murdoch, attention is an attitude entirely suited to the secular world. Do you live most fully by making the rock your thing (as Sisyphus does), by revolt, or by paying attention to the lives of others in an attitude that can only be called love – although perhaps the Latin *caritas* is more acute. Defined as affection, love, or esteem, the term connotes the value of the object loved rather than the intensity of desire. A Latin dictionary usually gives the first definition of *caritas* as "dearness" or "high price." In other words, *caritas* is distinct from Eros, which – as everyone from Plato to Freud knew – retains at its core a selfish element (Plato, *Symposium*, 203b–e; Freud 1930, 113–17). While the Greek Eros may be rendered by the Latin *amor*, *caritas* has a richer set of connotations than the Greek *philia*. The Greek *agape* comes close, but it is unnecessary to use a term so closely associated with Christian love.

An attitude of *caritas* toward the particulars of this world, what I have called attention, is one that renders this world sacred and holy – not in the sense that it belongs to God but rather in the sense that humans become capable of taking their everyday experiences with the things and people of this world and lifting them out of the mundane by an act of attention, or lucid concentration. In doing so, everyday experiences become for a moment numinous, set apart and special, worthy of our wonder and our awe. Paying attention renders the world we live in sacred, holy, and ablaze with meaning.

Contrast the attitude of attention with the world-weariness of Kohelet. Consider Kohelet's signature phrase, "there is nothing new under the sun" (Ecclesiastes 1:9, passim). Denizen of a world still new in Biblical time, history is already deep into its endless cycle as Kohelet experiences it. If one sees the world only in terms of mundane generalities, there *is* nothing new: men and women are born, live, suffer, try to grasp a little pleasure along the way – too often by denying it to others (as though that is how pleasure works) – and die. In fact, with every birth, with every glance, with every day something new is created under the sun. Newness appears when we look closely at something we thought we knew, only to see it in a novel light. Newness is the particular reframed. This experience of newness, discovered in the particular may itself be an experience of transcendence: transcendence on a small scale, even a human scale. I do not believe this is an oxymoron.

Like Kohelet, who is not comforted but besieged by the fact that the Lord "has set eternity in the hearts of men" (Ecclesiastes 3:11),

Camus would have nothing to do with an eternity that seems not so much to beckon as to tease:

I want everything to be explained to me or nothing.... What I fail to understand is nonsense.... If one could only say just once: 'This is clear,' all would be saved. (Camus 1955, 27)

Like Kohelet, the experience of being tempted by eternity stems (as all temptation does) from how much Camus wanted from the experience: not a moment in which his human categories are shattered but rather a knowledge that would be possible only from the perspective of eternity. Camus did not want to encounter eternity; he wanted to know it, master it, touch it – or he would know nothing. That could make life boring.

Paying attention to particular others is a back door to transcendence, sublimity in the dimension of the mundane. Like the transcendence Camus rejected, paying attention to others requires that we accept how little we will ever know about others, even those closest to us, allowing this knowledge-filled ignorance to fill us with awe. Paying attention to others requires on a human, everyday level precisely those qualities of modesty, ignorance, and openness to the mystery of otherness that will never be solved. Both Kohelet and Camus rejected transcendence when it comes to the big things, God and Eternity, because the experience is so limited, sometimes little more than a longing in the heart. This put them at risk of failing to pay attention to little things as well, for the logic is surprisingly similar: in both, we must give up the grasping desire to know, with no certainly (indeed, no likelihood) that our openness to experience will be rewarded with knowledge. Indeed, Kohelet was not merely at risk of failing to pay attention to everyday life; he succumbed to this risk. The result is boredom unto death.

Seen from a distance, everything looks the same. It's only up close that we can appreciate the particulars, that every life and every day is different. Only particularity overcomes entropy, finding newness in the smallest details. In a related fashion, Camus will know nothing if he can't know everything (this was not Camus's final position; he had none – it is a trope, a tendency, not a conclusion). This does not close Camus to an appreciation of the particulars of the world; without that appreciation, he would not have been the artist he was. However, he did not value particularity as he might have because he did not see singularity as worthy of worship in its own right. Sisyphus does, but surely his cultivated scorn must get in the way.

Levi, Camus, and George Orwell: A Conversation about Attention
Levi, Camus, and George Orwell each exemplify an aspect of attention; occasionally, they even seem to be having a conversation with each other. It is Camus's alter ego, Dr. Rieux, who says, "again and again there comes a time in history when the man who dares to say that two and two make four is punished with death" (1972, 125). He is talking about calling the plague "the plague." Similarly, it is Tarrou who says, "I'd come to realize that all our troubles spring from our failure to use plain, clean-cut language. So I resolved always to speak – and to act – quite clearly, as this was the only way of setting myself on the right track" (Camus 1972, 236).

Are these important links to Orwell or are they closer to coincidental literary tropes? (*La Peste* and Orwell's essay on "Politics and the English Language" [1970a] were originally published within a year of each other: 1947 and 1946.) Perhaps they are a little bit of both. What is truly important, the point that Orwell pursued that Camus did not, stems from what can only be regarded as a productive mistake in Orwell's literary vision: his windowpane theory of language.

Levi shared a similar view. In 1976, he initiated a public debate with the writer and literary critic, Giorgio Manganelli, when Levi published an article in *La Stampa* (1976) titled "On Obscure Writing":

In my opinion one should not write in an obscure manner, because a piece of writing has all the more value and all the hope of diffusion and permanence, the better it is understood and the less it lends itself to equivocal interpretations.... White pages are white, and it is best to call them white; if the king is naked, it is honest to say that he is naked. (Levi 1989, 170)

In response to Manganelli's reply, in which he accused Levi of acting as a literary "health and welfare" terrorist, Levi rejoined:

The belief that the written page is the symbol of the ultimate chaos to which we are doomed is an idea typical of our century.... I prefer to read someone who writes in a clear and luminous way. I prefer clarity to confusion. (Anissimov 2000, 323–4)

One difference between Levi and Orwell seems to be Levi's lesser concern with literature and politics per se and his greater concern with literary clarity as a means of warding off chaos of all kinds, including personal. His early biographer, Anissimov, pointed out that Levi reproached Georg Trakl and Paul Celan for their obscurity:

> ... daring to liken their poetry to the death rattle of a dying man. In Levi's view ... obscurity was a proto-withdrawal from the world, because both men had committed suicide. Though not unaware that there are elements of the unknowable and irrational in each of us, nevertheless he made the mistake of believing that clarity of speech could somehow ward them off. (Anissimov 2000, 252)

Orwell, on the other hand, was less concerned with chaos, whether of the metaphysical or psychological variety, and more concerned with the corruption of ordinary human decency by the corruption of language, be it the language of bureaucracy, doctrine, ideology, or academic life. In "Politics and the English Language," Orwell asserted that anyone who is not corrupted by these languages, anyone who just looks and sees, will know that kicking a coolie, procuring an abortion, abject and systematic poverty, and the destruction of natural beauty (to use four of Orwell's examples) are wrong.[5] Writing so clear and limpid that it seems to disappear, leaving only its subject, is the contribution intellectuals can make – perhaps their only contribution – to preventing doctrine, dogma, bureaucracy, laziness, and educated stupidity from getting in the way of ordinary human decency (Orwell 1970a).

The trouble is, today we know – or think we know – that Orwell's windowpane theory of language, language so limpid it lets us see reality with nothing added or subtracted, is just one more rhetorical strategy designed to create the illusion of objectivity, when it is, of course, the author who is creating the frame and form within which an infinitely interpretable reality is seen as objectively present to the reader.[6] Although certainly true, this insight hardly matters, at least

---

[5] Orwell's four examples are (in order) from a newspaper column written in 1940, recalling his first experience of Asia in 1922; *Keep the Aspidistra Flying*, *The Road to Wigan Pier*, and *Coming up for Air*.

[6] From Rorty, *Contingency, Irony, and Solidarity* (1989, 173–4). If we are looking at metaphors, Rorty said, then Orwell's writing, all persuasive writing, comes closer to

as far as Orwell was concerned. The key point is not the windowpane theory but rather Orwell's moral particularism (Orwell 1970b); they are related.

Pay attention to life as it goes on around you, pay attention to details, try to understand what they are, and how you stand in relationship to these details, empirically and morally. That is, make the links, preferably little links, not big ones: not globalization (which at its worst links everything to everything else, which is functionally equivalent to linking everything to nothing) but rather how do I stand in relation to the person who cleans my house, serves my food, begs on the corner? There is no reason not to make larger, more encompassing theoretical links as well, but it is too easy to use big abstract links to dissolve little concrete links, and so feel a little less: less responsible, less engaged – that is, just feel less. Theory also can obliterate the link between thought and feeling, the link that animates our words. Instead:

> ... observe closely what's going on around you; pay attention to its particulars and try to understand why they are what they are; you will often know when something you see or have proposed to you is offensive to the natural order; when you know this, protest it, remove your cooperation from it, refuse to listen to those who offer theoretical justifications of it, and do what you can to prevent if from continuing. This won't, thinks Orwell, solve all political and economic problems. Some can only be addressed at the theoretical level.... [But] In the kinds of cases that interest him, Orwell thinks that the clear eye can be sure that what is recommended is wrong – surer than the intellect can be of the upshot of any theoretical argument at a high level of abstraction. This conviction lies at the heart of an Orwellian epistemology. (Griffiths 2004, 38)

For Levi, one's commitment to attention stems from "the intrinsic dignity not only of people but also of things, of their own truth, which we should recognize and not distort if we do not wish to fall into the generic" (Levi 2005, 16). As suggested, this sounds much like Adorno's negative dialectics (mimesis), in which the object comes first, in which we resist the all-too-human tendency to subsume the object

---

a strategically placed lever than a windowpane, providing an alternative description of familiar events. Not, for example, "smoke pouring from mighty smokestacks" but "black soot covering the landscape."

to the concept. Instead, we respect the particularity of the object, people, and things (Adorno 1973, 44–7; 1978, 247). The difference is that Levi understood that our experience of nature, including human nature, will always be split: nature is maternal and nature is "hostile, violent, alien" (Levi 2002, 214):

> Matter is maternal, even etymologically, but it is also inimical. The same goes for nature. But man is matter and thus in conflict with himself, as all religions have acknowledged. Matter is also an education, a genuine school for life. Fighting against it, you mature and grow. In the course of the struggle, you win and you lose. At times matter seems astute, at others obtuse, and there's no contradiction because the two different aspects coexist. (Levi 2001b, 92)

Both facets of our experience of nature must be considered, which is why Levi saw no contradiction between reason as calculator of nature and reason as the careful appreciation of the particularity of people and things, not subjecting them to the tyranny of the concept. There is no contradiction because *this* contradiction mirrors the duality of the world almost perfectly.

Although Dr. Rieux, narrator of Camus's *The Plague*, lacks the philosophical two-dimensionality of Levi, his attitude toward the plague and disease generally reflects that of Levi. "Rieux believed himself to be on the right road – in fighting against creation as he found it" (Camus 1972, 120). What both Levi and Camus brought to this project is the recognition that nature remains hostile to human existence and that human survival is a collective task. One can only fight *la peste*, including "*la peste brune*" ("the brown plague," the term given to the German occupying forces), as men living under conditions fit for human beings.

Anyone who has read and remembers the conditions in Oran under the plague knows that conditions fit for humans may include terror and mass death at the hands of a capricious nature. Under these conditions, the men and women of Oran organized themselves into sanitation brigades, hospital volunteer squads, quarantine workers, and so forth. Anyone who has read *Survival in Auschwitz* knows that for the most part, human will faltered and failed (this was Levi's judgment) because the conditions were no longer fit for humans. This is not because the conditions in the Lager were more capricious than in

Oran (although they were certainly more brutal), but because humans had made them so and everyone knew it. This knowledge is the most demoralizing of all.

For Levi, paying attention is an unalloyed virtue, even if its connection to ordinary human decency is not as finely developed as it is in Orwell. What about Camus? For Camus, attention remains the quality of several characters in *The Plague*. It is not a theme that runs throughout his work.[7] Once, a much younger (twenty-three years old) Camus wrote that "the only thing that can defeat absurdity is lucidity." By *lucidity*, he meant something akin to what I am calling *attention*, although it was not quite clear whether Camus meant attention to one's *art* of expressing the daily humiliations of the poor and oppressed or attention to the lives of the poor and oppressed themselves (Todd 1997, 41–2). While both are important, attention as an act of veneration applies only to the latter. In any case, an older Camus would never have written about defeating absurdity, and neither should we.

Lucidity still has much to recommend it, however, and Levi was nothing if not lucid. For all that lucidity conceals (lucidity too is a rhetorical strategy because reality is not as clear as all that), everyday lucidity becomes more important. Not because the world is so complicated and must be simplified but because the world has become so intertextual, the world as wall-to-wall text, to use a wonderful image of the late Edward Said. In this world, the simple idea of paying attention to people and their lives, asking them what they are going through, what they might be suffering, is radical. To consider that it might even be an act of homage, or reverence, to the world and those who suffer it reminds us that paying attention is one of the simplest, most awesome, and respectful acts we can undertake.

What Does Paying Attention Have to Do with Transcendence?

This is neither the time nor the place to take up the dense, fascinating, and extensive body of work of Gilles Deleuze. However, a brief

---

[7] One might imagine that romantic love would lead to heightened attention. This theme too is present in *The Plague*. Even so, Camus (1972, 126) was more concerned with the loss of one's beloved, and The Fall from paradise that unending exile represents, than fascination with the qualities of one's beloved associated with romantic love. Not even the nostalgia that so captivated Camus (1955, 28) lingers on particularity. On the contrary, nostalgia lingers on images of lost wholeness and completeness.

essay written shortly before his death, "Immanence: A Life," raised the question of whether what I have called paying attention has anything to do with transcendence and, if so, what might transcendence mean? (Deleuze 2005, 25–33). The simplest statement about paying attention is that it has nothing to do with transcendence as it is normally understood. Paying attention does nothing to create new realities; that is, paying attention is not reality constitutive, the Kantian way of thinking about transcendence (Kant 1965, 118–19). Neither does paying attention lift us out of the plane of immanence, as Deleuze called it.

For Deleuze (2005, 25), as for so many Continental philosophers, the human subject disappears to be replaced by a "qualitative duration of consciousness without a self." If there is any sublimity to be had, then it is to be found in the delirium of singularity that takes the place of subjectivity, the presubjective delirium that is life (Rajchman 2005, 13). Although Peter Hallward (2006) went too far in arguing that Deleuze's philosophy is indifferent to the actual, material conditions of existence, it does seem as if Deleuze is more interested in the self's experience of itself in the world (even if this is now called transcendental empiricism rather than phenomenology) than in the self's experience of the world.[8]

If the simplest statement about paying attention is that it is not an instance of transcendence in any of the senses in which the term *transcendence* is normally understood, then the simplest statement about Deleuze is that he will not allow us to forget this fact. Deleuze turned Kant upside down, that favorite maneuver of philosophers. Instead of our concepts making experience possible, our experience exceeds our concepts, as novelty and difference force themselves on us, demanding that we come up with new categories lest we be overwhelmed. This is what Deleuze meant by transcendental empiricism.

"Is that really so far from what you are writing about?," the reader might ask. "Isn't it a type of sublimity of the particular?" If I were to say that paying attention to the particular takes us out of ourselves for a little while, while not taking us anywhere else, then my argument

---

[8] Deleuze's oeuvre is extensive. His collaborations with Pierre-Félix Guattari, particularly *Anti-Oedipus* (1983), resulted in a profound critique of late capitalism, whether or not one agrees with his conclusions. He did not ignore the world.

would come close in some ways to that of Deleuze. For this is where
Deleuze was headed, the ethics of self-creation:

Herein, perhaps, lies the secret: to bring into existence and not to judge. If
it is so disgusting to judge, it is not because everything is of equal value, but
on the contrary because what has value can be made or distinguished only by
defying judgment. What expert judgment, in art, could ever bear on the work
to come? (Deleuze 1997, 135)

However, I have added another consideration, one that begins with
Tarrou and continues through Orwell and Levi. Paying attention takes
us out of ourselves in order to share in some way – however limited,
however doomed to failure – the experiences of others by asking
the question the seeker asks the suffering king in Weil's version of
the legend of the Holy Grail: "What are you going through?" *That* is
paying attention. Attention turns us from ourselves, opening us to the
experiences of others, even if we can never have those experiences.

It would be gratuitous to claim that if someone had asked Levi this
question with the proper sincerity it would have saved his life. Not
for a second do I believe that it would. Nevertheless, there is a theme
that runs through the testimony of survivors and the work of Levi,
as well as being implicit in the silence of Job: "Nobody understands,
nobody could understand. How could they? I can't even believe it
myself." The attempt to understand others and their suffering, while
sometimes benefiting the one who suffers, surely must often enlarge
the world of one who would understand. Even if this does not ease
much suffering, a world with more understanding people can hardly
be a bad thing. Furthermore, it has been my experience (limited as
it is) that in attempting to understand the suffering of others, I have
become more attuned, not less, to the little beauties of everyday life.
If one wishes to argue that this means no more than that my iron cage
admits a little more light, so be it. If Deleuze reinforced that message
with a transcendental empirical hammer, that is all right too.

Finally, one might ask, how does what I am talking about differ from
the "transgression downward" to which Lang (2000, 56–7) referred, in
which the actual evil of Auschwitz overwhelms the imagination for evil?
The difference is that Lang was talking about concepts and historical
experiences on a vast (and horrific) scale, such as the Holocaust, and I
am talking about particular experiences. These experiences may well

concern pain and suffering, as Weil's story about asking the afflicted king what he is going through revealed. However, the experiences I am concerned with are individual, not general, not conceptual – or, rather, these encounters are about small concepts called experiences, not large ones called history, because all thinking is conceptual. Viewing the testimony of individual witnesses is an ideal place to pay attention to the particulars – if one can stand it.

Tohu Bohu

Let us begin with what seems to be Levi's definitive theological statement. The statement is toward the conclusion of *Survival in Auschwitz*, and says simply, "Today I think that if for no other reason than that an Auschwitz existed, no one in our age should speak of Providence" (1996, 157–8). (*"Oggi io penso che, se non altro per il fatto che un Auschwitz è esistito, nessuno dovrebbe ai nostri giorni parlare di Provvidenza"* [Levi 1958, 199].) In some respects, the statement is straightforward, capturing not only Levi's but also a generation's religious disillusionment. In other respects, there is nothing at all straightforward about the statement. Not to speak of Providence is not to deny it; not to speak of Providence in our age does not mean that humanity should never speak of it again.[9] Furthermore, the sentence that follows refers to the experience of the Russian liberation of the camps in terms of "the memory of biblical salvations in times of extreme adversity" that passed like a wind through all our minds.

Forty years later, a few months before his death, as he reread the typescript of an interview that contained these lines about Auschwitz and Providence, Levi added in pencil, "I find no solution to the riddle. I seek, but I do not find it" (Anissimov 2000, 183).

Although Levi does not frequently mention the Book of Job, the ovoid sphere with Job at the North Pole and Black Holes at the South defines not just Levi's readings, or even his life, but also his intellectual project. By the way, Black Holes had a double meaning for Levi, referring not only to the astrophysical phenomenon but also to the

---

9 The *New Shorter Oxford English Dictionary* defines *Providence*, especially when capitalized, as it is in both the Italian and English texts, as referring to the foreknowing and protective care of God, as in *Divine Providence*.

way in which Auschwitz itself was at risk of falling down the Black Hole of forgetfulness, the topic of a late (1987) op-ed piece of his titled "The Black Hole of Auschwitz" in *La Stampa* (Thomson 2002, 523).[10] By forgetting Auschwitz, Levi meant nothing so simple as the next generation's ignorance of the existence of the Holocaust. Levi was concerned, for example, that soon the Holocaust would be equated with equally murderous but nonetheless qualitatively different horrors, such as Stalin's mass murder of the Kulaks. This was the subject of his article in *La Stampa*.

Critics often comment on the frequency with which Levi alluded to Dante's *Divine Comedy*, especially in *Survival in Auschwitz*. Some see it as an organizing metaphor. Widely noticed but less frequently elaborated on is the centrality of Biblical images and references throughout Levi's work. One reason Levi's Biblical references evoke less commentary is likely because it is difficult to know how to take those references. Are they mere literary allusions? If not, then what? Consider the following observation on *The Reawakening*:

Levi, who often interweaves religious themes with equal liberty from either the Old Testament or the New Testament, always in a secular spirit, makes of Cesare a Christ-like figure. At the beginning of the story, Cesare's emaciated appearance is compared to that of Christ on the cross. (Patruno 1995, 40; Levi 1995, 74)

Against Cesare, Levi sets Mordo, a "wise serpent," who tempts Levi "in another scene reminiscent of Adam before The Fall, by offering him one of his women" (Patruno 1995, 47; Levi 1995, 53).

The first thing to note is the banality of the critic's comment, "always in a secular spirit," whatever that means. The second is that finding the right terms to characterize Levi's frequent use of Biblical allusions and references is not easy. Following are several of Levi's Biblical references out of dozens.

The tattooing of his number on arrival at Auschwitz is his "baptism" (Levi 1996, 27).

The stories the Lager inmates tell each other – all different and all the same, stories of suffering, loss, and subjection to necessity – are

---

[10] This double meaning appears to be lost in the recent translation of a collection of readings from Levi bearing the title *The Black Hole of Auschwitz* (2005). The Italian title of this collection is quite different, *L'asimmetria e la vita* (Torino: Einaudi, 2002). Levi believed that asymmetry was the key to life.

not just "like the stories of the Bible." They are more. "Are they not themselves stories of a new Bible?" (1996, 65–6). A book of suffering without redemption.

After the Germans fled Auschwitz, only the sick and dying remained in the *Revier*. Levi and several others found the strength to fetch a stove, cook a meal, and so create a human environment for themselves and a few others. About this accomplishment, he said, "We were broken by tiredness, but we seemed to have finally accomplished something useful – perhaps like God after the first day of creation" (1996, 160–1).

The Drowned and the Saved – the title Levi would have given to his first book, the title he finally gave to the last – although not an allusion to a particular passage in the Bible, refers to a frequent contrast. The suffering say they feel as though they are drowning in deep water (Psalm 69:1–2; Lamentations 3:54), whereas being saved from an enemy is likened to being pulled from the waters of death (Psalm 18:16).

Presumably, Levi was aware that his observation about survival in the Lager, "for he who has will be given . . . and the man who has not will forfeit even what he has," alludes to a saying of Jesus Christ (Levi 1988, 80–1; Matthew 13:12). Except that Levi was now doing more than using Biblical references and allusions; he was recontextualizing them so that they are fitting to a life in hell. This became more common in his later work. *Tohu bohu* is the culmination of this reversal, an image of creation transformed into the void of destruction.

Neither are all of Levi's religious references literary allusions. In struggling with the question of theodicy, he cannot avoid doing theology. For example, during October 1944, there was a great *selekeja*, a selection designed to reduce the numbers in the camp to prepare for new arrivals. After the selection in Levi's barracks, silence prevailed:

> . . . and then, from my bunk on the top row, I see and hear old Kuhn praying aloud, with his beret on his head, swaying backwards and forwards violently. Kuhn is thanking God because he has not been chosen. . . . Does he not see Beppo the Greek in the bunk next to him. Beppo who is twenty years old and is going to the gas chamber the day after tomorrow and knows it. . . . If I was God, I would spit at Kuhn's prayer. (Levi 1996, 129–30)

This is not a Biblical allusion. This is a statement about the proper theological attitude, one that Levi himself struggled to maintain. As Levi said in "God and I," an interview given in 1983, he too was tempted to pray during the great selection. He immediately said to himself, "No, you can't do this, you don't have the right. First, because you don't believe in God; second, because asking for favors, without having a special case, is the act of a *mafioso*" (Levi 2001b, 275).

One is tempted to say that these two sentences capture all that is important and apparently contradictory about Levi's belief in God. He didn't believe, but he continued to adhere to principles of right belief – above all, that a man, or at least a man like Levi, has no special claim on God's favor. No wonder Levi struggled with Auschwitz and God until the end of his days. He took seriously what he didn't believe, a principle not as contradictory as it sounds. For religious belief is not about how we conduct ourselves in relationship to a Supreme Being. Religious belief is about how we conduct ourselves in relationship to our idea of a Supreme Being. It is entirely possible, as Levi revealed, that this idea may be held in the subjunctive. "If there were a God, He would spit on Kuhn's prayer (as I would), and I would not pray to Him to be spared the selection, because I have no special merit above all the others, one of whom would have to take my place."

Levi never put it in quite those words. Generally, he found it easier to deny the existence of God – or, at least, a God who answers prayers because Levi found it quite easy to imagine a Creator, even One who continues to attend to His creation, but not to His human creatures (2001b, 276).

If this were all there was to Levi's theology, we would understand the persistence of the riddle that could not be solved – indeed, should not be solved, lest one of the two terms, *God* or *Auschwitz*, be trivialized. What would not be explained is the anguish this caused Levi. As a believer in a subjunctive God, Levi should have been able to do what he claimed to do: dismiss the problem with a lightly delivered "So I hold on to the simpler hypothesis: I deny him."

However, Levi *never* held to the simpler hypothesis, except perhaps to cloak the complexity of his beliefs. On the contrary, Levi looked for God even or perhaps especially in the midst of his despair. As he said in late 1983, "This is the fourth depression of my life. I want to end it. But the third floor is not high enough. . . . I was stronger in the Lager. . . . I'm looking for God, but I can't find him."[11]

---

[11] The source is the diary of Gisella, an intimate friend of Levi's during the last fifteen years of his life. She was known only to Carole Angier (2002, 655); no other biographer was aware of this source. Although Angier was convincing, Gisella is a sole

Levi couldn't find Him because he believed that Auschwitz represented the triumph of destruction over creation – not perhaps for all time, but for our age. This is the implication of *tohu bohu*, which comes to represent not an alternative account of creation but rather an account of destruction – not only of individuals but also of civilization.

That God created the universe *ex nihilo*, out of nothing, has been the received interpretation of Genesis 1:1–2 at least since Augustine, who held that God stands outside time. In creating the universe, God brings time and with it the possibility of causality and constraint into existence (*Confessions*, bk. XI, c. 12–14). God Himself stands outside of these conditions. Some theologians and philosophers reject creation *ex nihilo*, arguing that Genesis 1:2 clearly states that God created the universe *tohu wa-bohu*, out of the chaos of preexisting formless matter (Cobb and Griffin 1976, 54–67).[12]

The account of creation in the Book of Job is entirely compatible with the view that God struggled with matter to create the universe. Indeed, God is proud of His creation precisely *because* of the powerful autonomous forces He had to overcome.

Tohu bohu made its appearance in *The Drowned and the Saved* (1988), in which Levi used the term to describe the melding of physical and mental anguish among the inmates. It was, he said:

. . . an atavistic anguish whose echo one hears in the second verse of Genesis: the anguish inscribed in everyone of the "tohu-bohu" of a deserted and empty universe crushed under the spirit of God but from which the spirit of man is absent: not yet born or already extinguished. (85)

---

source, not the last word. It is the same Gisella who claimed that Levi called her on the Wednesday before his death on Saturday and said, "*Penso sola a sopprimermi*" ("I think only of killing myself") (Angier 2002, 728). By the way, the term *sopprimere* is somewhat unusual; it is the term one would normally use to refer to destroying a sick or injured animal. "*Suicidarsi*" is the usual Italian term for "to commit suicide."

[12] In the view of "process philosophy" as expressed by Whitehead's *Process and Reality* (1978), God should not be treated as an exception to metaphysical principles; otherwise, there can be no reasoned discourse about the divine. Whitehead never claimed to answer the "God question," as he called it. "There is merely the confrontation of the theoretic system with a certain rendering of the facts" (1978, 343). Whitehead believed, and said he was surprised to find himself believing, that the facts required a certain concept of God for their explanation, for he began his reflections on nature as an agnostic. In practice, Whitehead segued easily from being the disciplined philosopher to lyric theologian, writing in the same book that God does not create the world, He saves it – or, more accurately, "he is the poet of the world, with tender patience leading it by his vision of truth, beauty, and goodness" (1978, 346).

For Levi, *tohu bohu* referred not to creation and not to the limits of God but rather to destruction. *Tohu bohu* is the void of hopelessness and shame into which all who experienced Auschwitz are drawn, the shame of weakness and despair in a world in which there is no goodness left – a world in which God's presence is felt only as a crushing absence and humanity's failure a crushing defeat.

It is not unusual to find *tohu bohu* being used as a literary rather than a theological image. Certainly, one could argue that is the only sense in which Levi used the term here. It does not matter because Levi's point was the same whether he was doing theology or literary criticism (broadly interpreted), the same criticism he undertook in *The Search for Roots*, in which the diagram that opens the anthology represents an ovoid sphere with Job at the North Pole and Black Holes at the South (2002, 9). Connecting the poles are four meridians, each referring to a literary path that Levi has taken. Calvino (2002, 222), whose description of this graphic I have adopted throughout, referred to these four meridians as "four lines of resistance to all forms of despair, four responses that define his stoicism."

One might think about how little pressure is required for these lines of resistance, the lines of literature, the lines of civilization, to crack, so that the sphere collapses into itself, Job into the Black Holes, suffering into nothingness, without a glimmer of redemption. Certainly, this is where Levi seemed to end up. However, the situation is worse than that because the meridians are not really that at all. Calvino failed to mention a decisive point. If one looks closely, one sees that each apparent meridian is actually a curved arrow, with a point at only one end, leading in each case from Job to Black Holes. Passing through the marvelously diverse literature of Rabelis, T. S. Eliot, Darwin, Conrad, Sholem Aleichem, and Marco Polo, among others, in the end all paths lead to the Black Hole. There is no exit, no escape, and no detour, just a slightly curved path from unmerited, unwarranted suffering into an oblivion that will never be redeemed by God or man.

One does not want to read this diagram in this way, but there is no other choice, no way around it. One-way signs are not meridians (Calvino 2002, 222). Except that now we have some idea about why Levi felt so naked, so exposed in editing this collection of abridged readings. He was revealing the *tohu bohu* at the bottom of his heart, his conviction that at least in this time and this place destruction had triumphed, swallowing everything that makes life decent, humane, and civilized. Levi may have lived his literary life as the well-mannered cicerone of hell, as Ozick called him, but that only heightens by contrast what he knew: that we live in an era in which hell triumphed and that in the end, this is all our guide can teach us. I don't believe this is true. I believe that Levi believed it was true and his diagram was the closest he ever came to telling us what was at the bottom of his heart. It takes a little decoding, but not much.

A question remains. What about the truth of the Book of Job? What is this truth? That our suffering is meaningful, purposeful, and quite incomprehensible to us now and probably forever, until the end of time. Nevertheless, believing that one's suffering has a place and a purpose itself provides a meaning, a meaning that comes closer to the realm of awe than to comfort. About this possibility I have suggested that Levi took it more seriously than a casual reading of his work suggests. "I choose not to believe right now," as though the human signatory of the covenant had a choice. Given the history of the last century and God's apparent absence when He was most needed, withholding one's consent might make sense.

To be sure, it is God who makes covenants, God who chooses when and how to appear. About His name, Yahweh, Harold Bloom (2005, 128) told us that it may be read as a punning reference to his self-definition, "I am that I am," better translated as "I will be where and when I will be" (*ehyeh asher ehyeh*) (Exodus 3:14), which is almost as easily read as "I won't be where you want me to be and desperately need me to be." If so, and if one takes God as seriously as Levi did, then perhaps it makes sense to say, even as one risks the arrogance of Job (the Job who wants to take God to court), that in this time and in this place in history, it is too difficult to believe, too difficult to love God. There is no reason to reject this position as long as we remember that humans need to love God more than God needs to love humans. This has been true since the Book of Job, where God took if not His leave from man, then at least His most dramatic step back from His creation. God had hoped that by wantonly inflicting suffering on Job, He would provoke a greater, more glorious demonstration of Job's devotion to Him (Miles 1966, 404–6). Instead, Job will remain in awe of God, but that is not the same as fidelity and affection. If God turns out to be a rather stark and distant character, Job turns out to be a silent and mysterious one. Job will worship God, but will Job love Him?

A Cruel Reality Is Not Absurd

If there is any single lesson to be learned from listening to hour after hour of testimony by witnesses, it is that although the Holocaust was not a highly organized death machine, it was sufficiently well organized to give thousands of Germans, Poles, and others the opportunity to inflict their cruelty on defenseless, demoralized victims before killing them. If one allows the testimony of survivors to take the lead, putting aside what one thinks one knows about history and the plans of those who organized the Holocaust, one could almost think that the point was never merely to kill the victims but rather to torment them unto death.

Consider a fine book on the brutality of German killers, Christopher Browning's *Ordinary Men* (1993).[13] Unlike Arendt's *Eichmann in Jerusalem* (1965) with its thesis of the banality of evil, or the functionalist explanation of Hilberg's *The Destruction of the European Jews* (1985), Browning focused on the bloody brutality of Reserve Police Battalion 101, a group of older reservists. Browning posed the problem in terms of how these men managed to cope with the "burden of choice": kill old men, women, children, and babies at close range, becoming covered in the blood and brains of their victims; or step out and not participate, an opportunity they were explicitly offered by their unusual commanding officer, Major Wilhelm ("Papa") Trapp. No more than 10 percent ever stepped out, and perhaps 5 to 10 percent more drifted off into the woods during the mass killings. None from either group ever faced official reprimand or sanction for doing so.

Browning, like Hilberg, fell into the moderate functionalist camp, which means that he believed that the initiative for the "Final Solution" lay not primarily with Hitler but rather with those lower down the bureaucratic hierarchy. Intentionalists hold that the Holocaust was a top-down phenomenon. Unlike Hilberg, Browning's *Ordinary*

---

[13] The term *German* is used intentionally; most were not members of the *Nationalsozialistische Deutsche Arbeiterpartei* – that is, the Nazi Party.

Men is almost exclusively concerned with those who did the actual killing. If one were to label the position taken in this book, one might call it the survivor perspective: What does the Holocaust look like from the perspective of those who were its victims and lived to tell about it?

The survivor perspective is not comprehensive; it is not in competition with functionalist or even intentionalist explanations. It needs one or the other to make it complete. Recall the bad-fate (bad-*beshert*) explanation of Hanna T. in the last chapter, an explanation that cannot be allowed to stand on its own, even as it brings something important to our understanding of the Holocaust. As important is what survivors have to tell us about the behavior of their guards. Consider the testimony of Max B. (T-94), locked together with a hundred others in a boxcar with no water for days. Attempting to lower a cup attached to a string to catch a little snow to melt and drink, they soon gave up because the guards riding on top of the train shot at them and their swaying cup when they leaned out a tiny window as the train moved on slowly. Eventually, they were reduced to sipping their own urine. What if we read Max B.'s testimony, along with that of thousands of other survivors, not only as an account of abject souls but also as a theory of the Holocaust?

These lessons about the Holocaust are inscribed on the survivor's body, in his or her deep memory, in memories closer to sensations and images than words. Interpreted as a story about the world they survived, the testimony of witnesses is not just an explanation of what suffering can do to a man or a woman but also is an explanation of the apparent motives behind the men and women who caused the Holocaust – and, hence, an explanation, a partial explanation, of the Holocaust itself. We read the motive of the perpetrator in the body and soul of the tormented witness, but not just there. Many of the tormented can tell us in words – if, that is, we avoid turning the witness into our only subject.

Germans – in this case, the SS (*Schutzstaffel*) according to Max B. – participated in the Holocaust because sadistic acts like these gave them pleasure. This explanation is more in line with a functionalist explanation, but it is not incompatible with an intentionalist explanation. Organized and directed from the top down by Hitler, Himmler, and a few others, the Holocaust provided an opportunity for ordinary sadists such as Max B.'s guards to indulge their capricious cruelty. The same holds true for extraordinary sadists, such as Josef Mengele, whose cruelty was systematic. "In ordinary times he could have been a slightly sadistic German professor" is how one perceptive survivor of Auschwitz-Birkenau characterized Mengele (Lifton 1986, 377). Auschwitz was an outlet, a release – not a cause.

Analyzing the situation of the ordinary men of Police Battalion 101, Browning (1993, 167–76) wondered if it was like a real-life Milgram (1974) experiment in the forests of Poland, referring to the famous psychological study in which an experimenter ordered ordinary men and women to deliver what they believed were painful, quite possibly fatal electrical shocks to a mild-mannered man with a heart condition whom they heard screaming for his life. Most complied with the experimenter's orders. Or, was the situation of these ordinary men more akin to the Zimbardo experiment, as it is called, in which sociologists constructed a simulated prison on the campus of Stanford University, recruiting students to act as guards and prisoners for a period of two weeks? The experiment was terminated in less than a week because the guards, acting under no authority but their own, became increasingly imaginative in their cruelty, as one prisoner put it during a debriefing (Zimbardo et al. 1983).[14] Was there an implicit authority structure that led Browning's ordinary men to murder innocents, even as they were given the unusual permission to defer? Or, were these ordinary killers the subjects of group pressure, peer pressure, as we call it today? In either case, Browning (1993, 188–9), Milgram, and Zimbardo seem agreed on one thing:

Our results are also congruent with those of Milgram who most convincingly demonstrated the proposition that evil acts are not necessarily the deeds of evil men, but may be attributable to the operation of powerful social forces. . . . The

---

[14] Zimbardo et al. (1983) argued that the power of the experiment stems from the fact that the subjects were screened in advance, subjected to a battery of paper and pencil psychological tests, to remove from the pool all who scored beyond the normal on measures of the authoritarian personality and other criteria. The self-selection hypothesis, which might apply to the SS, does not apply here. The "prisoner's" comment about the "guards'" imagination for cruelty appears in a film Zimbardo made about the experiment, in which he brought prisoners and guards together a number of weeks after the experiment.

inherently pathological characteristics of the . . . situation itself . . . were a sufficient condition to produce aberrant, anti-social behavior. (Zimbardo et al. 1983, 90)[15]

I cannot prove that the "social forces" explanation is insufficient, but it is certainly not a proposition demonstrated by Milgram nor anyone else, for that matter, including Browning (1993), who concluded his book with these lines: "Within virtually every social collective, the peer group exerts enormous pressures on behavior and sets moral norms. If the men of Reserve Police Battalion 101 could become killers under such circumstances, what group of men cannot?" (189).

What seems to have happened is that a question of perspective has become one of definition. The question is whether to focus on the social forces that release sadism and cruelty or on the sadism and cruelty that are evidently just lying in wait, ready to be released. More explicitly than most (although the reasoning is the same), Zygmunt Bauman transformed this question of perspective into one of definition in *Modernity and the Holocaust* (1989):

And yet, clearly and unambiguously, the orgy of cruelty that took Zimbardo and his colleagues by surprise, stemmed from a vicious social arrangement, and not from the viciousness of the participants. Were the subjects of the experiment assigned to the opposite roles, the overall result would not be different. What mattered was the existence of a polarity, and not who was allocated to its respective sides. *What did matter was that some people were given a total, exclusive and untempered power over some other people.* (167–8, author's emphasis)[16]

---

[15] Browning would not absolve these ordinary murderers so readily, but he too looked to social forces and psychological strain, not pleasure in destruction, for his answer. The subtitle of Goldhagen's (1996) book, *Hitler's Willing Executioners: Ordinary Germans and the Holocaust*, is a deliberate swipe at Browning. Subsequent debate between them bears this out. See the transcript of "The 'Willing Executioners'/'Ordinary Men' Debate," with Daniel J. Goldhagen, Christopher R. Browning, and Leon Wieseltier (1996).

[16] Bauman offered no historical or empirical evidence for this assertion, only the claim that what he saw as the counterargument, "the authoritarian personality," amounts to little more than saying that Nazis were cruel because cruel people became Nazis (1989, 153). True enough, but assertion set against tautology is not intellectual progress. History, including the everyday history of testimony and memoir, is what is needed.

Because Bauman, like Browning, understood the Zimbardo experiment as a model of the psychological forces at work in the Holocaust, the first thing to say is that we don't know what would happen if the situations were reversed. History is not a laboratory. The idea of Jews, gypsies, homosexuals, and others having total control over the Germans is virtually unimaginable; any suggestion that the relationship between Israel and Palestine today resembles that experiment is obscene.

The second and more important point is that the value of testimony leads us to look at the other half of the definition, so to speak. If most studies look at the social forces that release cruelty, because that is what studies do – they look at social forces – then testimony leads us to focus on the cruelty itself. When one listens to the testimony of witnesses, one hears of an entirely different world than the one described by Browning: not one of conflicted men reluctant to kill but of men who seemed to take pleasure in inflicting a cruel death, and many more who actively supported it. Perhaps it is simply a difference in perspective (which end of the rifle or truncheon one happens to be on), but one wonders. Why listen to survivors so attentively when they tell us about their broken lives but not when they tell us the most obvious thing of all? Tens of thousands of men and thousands of women eagerly tormented, tortured, terrified, and degraded them and would have killed them all if they could – this while millions more looked on, uttering not one word of condemnation.

If this is true, then a social forces explanation of whatever kind is inadequate. Instead, tens of thousands of Germans, Poles, and others brought to the job an eagerness for cruelty and a lust for brutal dominion. Although I cannot prove that this is true, I can point to the testimony of thousands of survivors whose stories are inexplicable unless this is true – inexplicable in the sense that what they suffered is in no way matched by the social forces arrayed against them. Once one inhabits, or populates, those social forces with the sadism, hatred, and cruelty experienced by survivors, then the inexplicable becomes explicable. Not because every act of suffering and loss, even at human hands, is matched by a corresponding evil; the world is not in moral (or even immoral) balance. Arendt's (1965) banality of evil sometimes applies; certainly, it is not a concept to be banned in principle.

However, because the stories told by witnesses are for the most part stories about torment, torture, degradation, cruelty, and terror, they make sense only when these facts are put at the center of explanation as well as experience.

Once one does so, something interesting happens. Auschwitz becomes a little less absurd. Finally, *hier gibt es ein Warum.* Finally, here is an answer – not an answer that brings peace to the spirit, the peace that Levi mistakenly made the standard for a satisfactory answer for both the Holocaust and the torments of Job (Levi 2005, 61–2). Far from it. It is an answer that sends a shiver down the spine but it is an answer nonetheless. One reason Auschwitz happened in the way it did is because many (but not all) Germans and others in positions of authority found pleasure in subjecting their victims to a long drawn-out period of torment and torture before finally killing them, like a cat playing with a wounded mouse. Once we accept this as being a significant part of the story, Auschwitz as a leading site of absurdity becomes a little less absurd, as we recognize that by any standards of decent humanity there is something insane or evil at the heart of many (but not all) humans, waiting for a chance to emerge. A fog of confusion lifts just a little, as we let ourselves know what is so blindingly apparent that we could not see.

The result is that surplus absurdity becomes surplus sadism, surplus cruelty, surplus dominion – whatever one wants to call it; the name is not important. What is important is that we can begin to call things by their right name, even if there is no one right name (there is no essence of Auschwitz), only a range of possibilities. Furthermore, the term *surplus* takes on a new metaphorical meaning, signifying a surplus commodity in storage, just waiting to be drawn on by those in power when it is convenient to do so and the social situation is ripe.

We began with the Book of Job and what his affliction might teach us about a God still new and full of wonder at His creation. We should view the testimony of witnesses in the same spirit. They are our teachers and, like all good teachers, they teach us much about themselves and even more about the world. It is not unlike the problem of transcendence. Witnesses want to point beyond themselves to the world in which men and women did such terrible things. Those who watch and listen tend to remain stuck at the level of the subjectivity of the subject, not wanting to hear the content as much as analyze the one who bears the historical message inscribed on his or her wounded soul. Perhaps doing so is strangely more tolerable. Is it somehow easier to know about the hurt and humiliation of the wounded than the enthusiasm of those who inflicted it? Certainly, knowledge of this hurt and humiliation is more conceptually confined, more subject to theorizing. I have done my share. However, knowledge of the wounded subject is not more important than knowledge of what he or she would teach us about the world. Both are important. The interaction between the two is the most important of all, for it is where this knowledge resides.

Certainly, this is true about survivors, but it is also true about the silence of Job after his restoration, which encourages us to use our imagination to fill in the gaps. Is it not also true about Levi, who seems such a straightforward narrator, until we look closely and realize that we hardly knew the man at all? About Levi, I've made some guesses about how he might have become who he was, but that is all they will ever be and all they need to be, as long as the guesses also point us beyond Levi to his tormentors. He would have us do that.

References

Quotations from the Book of Job are generally from the *Oxford New English Bible*, occasionally from Scheindlin's (1998) translation, and at least once from the *King James Version*. Because references are given by chapter and verse, readers may consult their favorite translation. References to other classical sources are given in the text in the form that is typical for classical studies.

Adorno, Theodor. 1967. *Prisms*. Translated by Samuel Weber and Shierry Weber. Cambridge, MA: MIT Press.

Adorno, Theodor. 1973. *Negative Dialectics*. Translated by E. B. Ashton. New York: Seabury Press.

Amato, Joseph. 1975. *Mounier and Maritain: A French Catholic Understanding of the Modern World*. Ypsilanti, MI: Sapientia Press.

American Psychiatric Association. 2000. *Diagnostic and Statistical Manual of Mental Disorders*, Fourth Edition, Text Revision. Washington, DC: American Psychiatric Publishing.

Améry, Jean. 1980. *At the Mind's Limits: Contemplations by a Survivor on Auschwitz and Its Realities*. Translated by Sidney Rosenfeld and Stella P. Rosenfeld. Bloomington: Indiana University Press.

Angier, Carole. 2002. *The Double Bond: The Life of Primo Levi*. New York: Farrar, Straus and Giroux.

Anissimov, Myriam. 2000. *Primo Levi: Tragedy of an Optimist*. Translated by Steve Cox. Woodstock, NY: Overlook Press.

Arendt, Hannah. 1965. *Eichmann in Jerusalem: A Report on the Banality of Evil*, Revised and Enlarged Edition. New York: Viking Press.

Arendt, Hannah. 1968. "Isak Dinesen." In *Men in Dark Times*, pp. 95–110. New York: Harcourt, Brace and World.

Arendt, Hannah. 1973. *The Origins of Totalitarianism*, New Edition. New York: Harcourt, Brace and Company.

Bauman, Zygmunt. 1989. *Modernity and the Holocaust.* Ithaca, NY: Cornell University Press.

Benedict, Ruth. 1946. *The Chrysanthemum and the Sword: Patterns of Japanese Culture.* Boston: Houghton Mifflin.

Bettelheim, Bruno. 1943. "Individual and Mass Behavior in Extreme Situations." *Journal of Abnormal and Social Psychology,* 38: 417–62.

Bettelheim, Bruno. 1946. "Affidavit of Bruno Bettelheim Concerning Patterns of Adaptation of Concentration Camp Inmates." *Nazi Conspiracy and Aggression,* vol. 7 (Document L-73). Washington, DC: U.S. Government Printing Office. Available at www.uwe.ac.uk/genocide/concentration%20camps1.htm>.

Blanchot, Maurice. 1995. *The Writing of the Disaster.* Translated by Ann Smock. Lincoln: University of Nebraska Press.

Bloom, Harold. 2005. *Jesus and Yahweh: The Names Divine.* New York: Riverhead Books/Penguin.

Botwinick, Sara. 2000. "Aging After Surviving: How Religious Holocaust Survivors Cope with Their Trauma." *Journal of Jewish Communal Service,* 76: 228–35.

Browning, Christopher. 1993. *Ordinary Men: Reserve Police Battalion 101 and the Final Solution in Poland.* New York: Harper.

Calvino, Italo. 2002. "Afterword: The Four Paths of Primo Levi." In *The Search for Roots: A Personal Anthology,* by Primo Levi, pp. 221–4. Translated by Peter Forbes. Chicago: Ivan R. Dee, Publisher.

Camus, Albert. 1942. *Le Mythe de Sisyphe.* Paris: Librairie Gallimard, Nouvelle Edition.

Camus, Albert. 1955. *The Myth of Sisyphus and Other Essays.* Translated by Justin O'Brien. New York: Vintage Books.

Camus, Albert. 1968. *Lyrical and Critical Essays.* Translated by Ellen Conroy Kennedy. New York: Vintage Books.

Camus, Albert. 1972. *The Plague.* Translated by Stuart Gilbert. New York: Vintage Books.

Chesterton, G. K. 1916. "Introduction to the Book of Job." London: Cecil Palmer and Hayward. Available at www.dur.ac.uk/martin.ward/gkc/books/job.html.

Cobb, John B., Jr., and Griffin, David Ray. 1976. *Process Theology: An Introductory Exposition.* Louisville, KY: Westminster/John Knox Press.

Conradi, Peter J. 2001. *Iris Murdoch: A Life.* New York: W. W. Norton.

Delbo, Charlotte. 1995. *Auschwitz and After.* Translated by Rosette Lamont. New Haven, CT: Yale University Press.

Delbo, Charlotte. 2001. *Days and Memory.* Translated by Rosette Lamont. Evanston, IL: Marlboro Press/Northwestern University Press.

Deleuze, Gilles. 1997. "To Have Done with Judgment." In *Essays Critical and Clinical,* pp. 126–35. Translated by Daniel Smith and Michael Greco. Minneapolis: University of Minnesota Press.

Deleuze, Gilles. 2005. "Immanence: A Life." In *Pure Immanence: Essays on A Life,* pp. 25–33. Translated by Anne Boyman. New York: Zone Books.

Deleuze, Gilles, and Guattari, Pierre-Félix. 1983. *Anti-Oedipus: Capitalism and Schizophrenia.* Translated by Robert Hurley, Mark Seem, and Helen Lane. Minneapolis: University of Minnesota Press.

Eliot, T. S. 1950. *The Cocktail Party.* New York: Harcourt, Brace and World.

Elshtain, Jean Bethke. 1995. *Augustine and the Limits of Politics.* Notre Dame: University of Notre Dame Press.

Forbes, Peter. 2002. "Introduction" to *The Search for Roots: A Personal Anthology* by Primo Levi. Translated by Peter Forbes. Chicago: Ivan R. Dee, Publisher.

Freud, Anna. 1966. "Identification with the Aggressor." In *The Ego and the Mechanisms of Defense*, pp. 109–21. Translated by Cecil Baines. New York: International Universities Press, Revised Edition [volume 2 of *The Writings of Anna Freud*].

Freud, Sigmund. 1900. "The Interpretation of Dreams." In *The Standard Edition of the Complete Psychological Works of Sigmund Freud.* Edited by James Strachey, 24 volumes, vols. 4 and 5. London: Hogarth Press, 1953–1974.

Freud, Sigmund. 1910. "Leonardo da Vinci and a Memory of His Childhood." In *The Standard Edition*, vol. 11: 57–137.

Freud, Sigmund. 1912. "Totem and Taboo." In *The Standard Edition*, vol. 13: 1–163.

Freud, Sigmund. 1914. "The Moses of Michelangelo." In *The Standard Edition*, vol. 13: 211–38.

Freud, Sigmund. 1920. "Beyond the Pleasure Principle." In *The Standard Edition*, vol. 18: 3–64.

Freud, Sigmund. 1927. "The Future of an Illusion." In *The Standard Edition*, vol. 21: 1–56.

Freud, Sigmund. 1930. "Civilization and Its Discontents." In *The Standard Edition*, vol. 21: 59–145.

Friedlander, Saul. 1993. *Memory, History, and the Extermination of the Jews of Europe.* Bloomington: Indiana University Press.

Gambetta, Diego. 1999. "Primo Levi's Last Moments." In *The Boston Review*, vol. 24, no. 3 (Summer). Available at bostonreview.net/BR24.3/gambetta.html [the Internet version contains a "Postscriptum" dated April 2005].

Gilkey, Langdon. 2001. *On Niebuhr: A Theological Study.* Chicago: University of Chicago Press.

Girard, René. 1977. *Violence and the Sacred.* Translated by Patrick Gregory. Baltimore, MD: Johns Hopkins University Press.

Glass, James. 2004. *Jewish Resistance During the Holocaust: Moral Uses of Violence and Will.* New York: Palgrave Macmillan.

Goldhagen, Daniel Jonah. 1996. *Hitler's Willing Executioners: Ordinary Germans and the Holocaust.* New York: Knopf.

Goldhagen, Daniel J., Browning, Christopher R., and Wieseltier, Leon. 1996. "The 'Willing Executioners'/'Ordinary Men' Debate." Introduction by Michael Berenbaum. Available at http://www.ushmm.org/research/center/publications/occasional/1996-01/paper.pdf.

Gray, Francine du Plessix. 2001. *Simone Weil.* New York: Penguin.

Greenspan, Henry. 1998. *On Listening to Holocaust Survivors: Recounting and Life History.* Westport, CT: Praeger.

Griffin, David Ray. 1981. "Creation Out of Chaos and the Problem of Evil." In *Encountering Evil: Live Options in Theodicy*, pp. 101–36. Edited by Stephen T. Davis. Atlanta, GA: John Knox Press.

Griffiths, Paul J. 2004. "Orwell for Christians." *First Things*, December, no. 148: 32–40.

Gutiérrez, Gustavo. 2003. *On Job: God-Talk and the Suffering of the Innocent*. Translated by Matthew J. O'Connell. New York: Orbis Books.

Hallward, Peter. 2006. *Out of This World: Deleuze and the Philosophy of Creation*. London: Verso.

Hasker, William. 1998. *God, Time, and Knowledge*. Ithaca, NY: Cornell University Press.

Hilberg, Raul. 1985. *The Destruction of the European Jews*. New York: Holmes and Meier.

Honneth, Axel. 2008. *Reification: A New Look at an Old Idea*. Edited by Martin Jay, with commentaries by Judith Butler, Raymond Geuss, and Jonathan Lear. New York: Oxford University Press.

Horkheimer, Max, and Adorno, Theodor. 2002. *Dialectic of Enlightenment*. Translated by Edmund Jephcott. Stanford, CA: Stanford University Press.

Ionesco, Eugène. 1962. *Exit the King and Other Plays*. Translated by Donald Watson. New York: Grove Press.

Ionesco, Eugène. 2007. *The Bald Soprano and The Lesson – Two Plays*. Translated by Tina Howe. New York: Grove Press.

Jones, James W. 1991. *Contemporary Psychoanalysis and Religion: Transference and Transcendence*. New Haven, CT: Yale University Press.

Kant, Immanuel. 1965. *Critique of Pure Reason*. Translated by Norman Kemp Smith. New York: St. Martin's Press.

Kant, Immanuel. 1987. *Critique of Judgment: Including the First Introduction*. Translated by Werner S. Pluhar. Indianapolis, IN: Hackett.

Kierkegaard, Søren. 1957. *The Concept of Dread*. Translated by Walter Lowrie. Princeton, NJ: Princeton University Press.

Kierkegaard, Søren. 1985. *Fear and Trembling*. Translated by Alastair Hannay. New York: Penguin Books.

Klein, Melanie. 1975. "A Contribution to the Psychogenesis of Manic-Depressive States." In *Love, Guilt and Reparation and Other Works, 1921–1945*, pp. 262–89. New York: The Free Press [volume 1 of *The Writings of Melanie Klein*].

Kraft, Robert. 2002. *Memory Perceived: Recalling the Holocaust*. Westport, CT: Praeger.

Kristeva, Julia. 1982. *Powers of Horror: An Essay on Abjection*. Translated by Leon Roudiez. New York: Columbia University Press.

Kristeva, Julia. 1984. *The Revolution in Poetic Language*. Translated by Margaret Waller. New York: Columbia University Press [contains just over one-third of the French original, published in 1974, *La Rèvolution du langage poétique*].

Kristeva, Julia. 1987. *Tales of Love*. Translated by Leon Roudiez. New York: Columbia University Press.

Kristeva, Julia. 1989. *Black Sun: Depression and Melancholia.* Translated by Leon Roudiez. New York: Columbia University Press.

Kristeva, Julia. 1996. *Interviews.* Edited by Ross Guberman. New York: Columbia University Press.

Lacan, Jacques. 1977. *Écrits: A Selection.* Translated with an Introduction by Alan Sheridan. New York: W. W. Norton [page reference in text is to the Introduction by Sheridan].

Lang, Berel. 2000. *Holocaust Representation: Art within the Limits of History and Ethics.* Baltimore, MD: Johns Hopkins University Press.

Langer, Lawrence. 1978. *The Age of Atrocity: Death in Modern Literature.* Boston: Beacon Press.

Langer, Lawrence. 1980. "The Dilemma of Choice in the Death Camps." *Centerpoint: A Journal of Interdisciplinary Studies*, vol. 4, no. 1: 53–9.

Langer, Lawrence. 1991. *Holocaust Testimonies: The Ruins of Memory.* New Haven, CT: Yale University Press.

Laub, Dori. 1992a. "Bearing Witness, or the Vicissitudes of Listening." In *Testimony: Crises of Witnessing in Literature, Psychoanalysis, and History*, pp. 57–74. By Shoshana Felman and Dori Laub, MD. New York: Routledge.

Laub, Dori. 1992b. "An Event without a Witness: Truth, Testimony and Survival." In *Testimony: Crises of Witnessing in Literature, Psychoanalysis, and History*, pp. 75–92. By Shoshana Felman and Dori Laub, MD. New York: Routledge.

Lengyel, Olga. 1995. *Five Chimneys: A Woman Survivor's True Story of Auschwitz*, Second Revised Edition. Chicago: Academy Chicago Publishers.

Levi, Primo. 1958. *Se questo è un uomo.* Torino: Einaudi [Italian edition of the book translated into English in the United States as *Survival in Auschwitz*].

Levi, Primo. 1984. *The Periodic Table.* Translated by Raymond Rosenthal. New York: Schocken Books.

Levi, Primo. 1988. *The Drowned and the Saved.* Translated by Raymond Rosenthal. New York: Vintage.

Levi, Primo. 1989. *Other People's Trades.* Translated by Raymond Rosenthal. New York: Summit Books.

Levi, Primo. 1995. *The Reawakening.* Translated by Stuart Woolf. New York: Touchstone Books.

Levi, Primo. 1996. *Survival in Auschwitz: The Nazi Assault on Humanity.* Translated by Stuart Woolf. New York: Touchstone Books. [Includes Philip Roth's interview with Levi].

Levi, Primo. 2001a. "A Man Saved by His Skills." In *The Voice of Memory: Primo Levi Interviews, 1961–1987*, pp. 13–22. Edited by Marco Belpoliti and Robert Gordon. New York: The New Press [Interview with Philip Roth, 1986].

Levi, Primo. 2001b. *The Voice of Memory: Primo Levi Interviews, 1961–1987*, Edited by Marco Belpoliti and Robert Gordon. New York: The New Press.

Levi, Primo. 2002. *The Search for Roots: A Personal Anthology.* Translated by Peter Forbes. Chicago: Ivan R. Dee, Publisher.

Levi, Primo. 2005. *The Black Hole of Auschwitz.* Edited by Marco Belpoliti, translated by Sharon Wood. Malden, MA: Polity Press.

Lifton, Robert Jay. 1986. *The Nazi Doctors: Medical Killing and the Psychology of Genocide*. New York: Basic Books.

Macklin, Elizabeth. 1987. "Talk of the Town." *The New Yorker*, May 11: 32.

Marcuse, Herbert. 1966. *Eros and Civilization: A Philosophical Inquiry into Freud*. Boston: Beacon Press.

Marcuse, Herbert. 1978. *The Aesthetic Dimension*. Boston, MA: Beacon Press.

Maritain, Jacques. 1929. *Three Reformers: Luther, Descartes, Rousseau*. New York: Charles Scribner's Sons.

Maritain, Raïssa. 1961. *The Memoirs of Raïssa Maritain*. Translated by Julie Kernan. Garden City, NY: Doubleday.

McAfee, Noëlle. 2004. *Julia Kristeva*. New York and London: Routledge.

Miles, Jack. 1996. *God: A Biography*. New York: Vintage.

Milgram, Stanley. 1974. *Obedience to Authority: An Experimental View*. New York: Harper and Row.

Murdoch, Iris. 1970. *The Sovereignty of Good*. London: Routledge.

Murdoch, Iris. 1999. "The Sublime and the Good." In *Existentialists and Mystics: Writings on Philosophy and Literature*, pp. 205–20. Edited by Peter Conradi. New York: Penguin Books.

Neisser, Ulric. 1994. "Self-Narratives: True and False." In *The Remembering Self*. Edited by Ulric Neisser and Robyn Fivush. New York: Cambridge University Press.

Nietzsche, Friedrich. 1968a. *On the Genealogy of Morals*. In *Basic Writings of* Nietzsche, pp. 439–602. Translated by Walter Kaufmann. New York: Modern Library.

Nietzsche, Friedrich. 1968b. *The Birth of Tragedy out of the Spirit of Music*. In *Basic Writings of Nietzsche*, pp. 3–144. Translated by Walter Kaufmann. New York: Modern Library.

Nietzsche, Friedrich. 1974. *The Gay Science*. Translated by Walter Kaufmann. New York: Vintage Books.

Nussbaum, Martha. 1986. *The Fragility of Goodness: Luck and Ethics in Greek Tragedy and Philosophy*. Cambridge, UK: Cambridge University Press.

O'Brien, Conor Cruise. 1970. *Albert Camus of Europe and Africa*. New York: Viking.

Ofer, Dalia, and Weitzman, Lenore. 1998. *Women in the Holocaust*. New Haven, CT: Yale University Press.

Oliver, Kelly. 2002. "Introduction: Kristeva's Revolutions." In *The Portable Kristeva*. Edited by Kelly Oliver. New York: Columbia University Press [Updated Edition].

Orwell, George. 1949. *Nineteen Eighty-Four*. New York: Signet.

Orwell, George. 1970a. "Politics and the English Language." In *A Collection of Essays*, pp. 156–70. New York: Harcourt [original 1946].

Orwell, George. 1970b. "Why I Write." In *A Collection of Essays*, pp. 309–16. New York: Harcourt [original 1946].

Ozick, Cynthia. 1989. "Primo Levi's Suicide Note." In *Metaphor and Memory*, pp. 34–48. New York: Knopf.

Panichas, George. 1977. "Paths of Meditation." In *The Simone Weil Reader*, pp. 399–407. Edited by Panichas. Wakefield, RI: Moyer Bell.

Patruno, Nicholas. 1995. *Understanding Primo Levi*. Columbia: University of South Carolina Press.

Phillips, Adam. 1988. *Winnicott*. Cambridge, MA: Harvard University Press.

Rajchman, John. 2005. "Introduction" to *Pure Immanence: Essays on a Life*, by Gilles Deleuze, pp. 7–23. Translated by Anne Boyman. New York: Zone Books.

Rilke, Rainer Maria. 2000. *Duino Elegies: A Bilingual Edition*. Translated by Edward Snow. New York: North Point Press.

Rorty, Richard. 1989. *Contingency, Irony, and Solidarity*. Cambridge, UK: Cambridge University Press.

Roth, Philip. 2007. *Exit Ghost*. New York: Houghton Mifflin.

Sartre, Jean-Paul. 1964. *Nausea*. Translated by Lloyd Alexander. New York: New Directions.

Scarry, Elaine. 1985. *The Body in Pain: The Making and Unmaking of the World*. New York: Oxford University Press.

Scheindlin, Raymond. 1998. "Introduction" to *The Book of Job*. Translated by Raymond Scheindlin. New York: W. W. Norton.

Shklar, Judith. 1989. "The Liberalism of Fear." In *Liberalism and the Moral Life*, pp. 21–38. Edited by Nancy Rosenblum. Cambridge, MA: Harvard University Press.

Simpson, Mona. 2007. "If This Is a Man." *The Atlantic*, volume 299, no. 5 (June): 114–18.

Stanley, John L. 1987. "Is Totalitarianism a New Phenomenon? Reflections on Hannah Arendt's *Origins of Totalitarianism*." *The Review of Politics*, volume 49, no. 2: 177–207.

Taylor, Charles. 1989. *Sources of the Self: The Making of the Modern Identity*. Cambridge, MA: Harvard University Press.

Thomson, Ian. 2002. *Primo Levi: A Life*. New York: Henry Holt.

Todd, Oliver. 1997. *Albert Camus: A Life*. Translated by Benjamin Ivry. New York: Carroll and Graf.

Ulanov, Ann Belford. 2001. *Finding Space: Winnicott, God, and Psychic Reality*. Louisville, KY: Westminster/John Knox Press.

Weber, Max. 1958a. "Science as a Vocation." In *From Max Weber: Essays in Sociology*, pp. 129–56. Translated and edited by H. H. Gerth and C. Wright Mills. New York: Oxford University Press.

Weber, Max. 1958b. *The Protestant Ethic and the Spirit of Capitalism*. Translated by Talcott Parsons. New York: Charles Scribner's Sons.

Weber, Max. 1958c. "Religious Rejections of the World and Their Directions." In *From Max Weber: Essays in Sociology*, pp. 323–59. Translated and edited by H. H. Gerth and C. Wright Mills. New York: Oxford University Press.

Weil, Simone. 1963. *Gravity and Grace*. Translated by Emma Craufurd. New York and London: Routledge.

Weil, Simone. 1977a. "The Love of God and Affliction." In *The Simone Weil Reader*, pp. 439–68. Edited by George Panichas. Wakefield, RI: Moyer Bell.

Weil, Simone. 1977b. "The *Iliad*, Poem of Might." In *The Simone Weil Reader*, pp. 153–83. Edited by George Panichas. Wakefield, RI: Moyer Bell.

Weil, Simone. 1977c. "Reflections on the Right Use of School Studies with a View to the Love of God." In *The Simone Weil Reader*, pp. 44–52. Edited by George Panichas. Wakefield, RI: Moyer Bell.

Weil, Simone. 1977d. "Metaxu." In *The Simone Weil Reader*, pp. 363–5. Edited by George Panichas. Wakefield, RI: Moyer Bell.

Weissman, Gary. 2004. *Fantasies of Witnessing: Postwar Efforts to Experience the Holocaust.* Ithaca, NY: Cornell University Press.

Whitehead, Alfred North. 1978. *Process and Reality.* Edited by David Ray Griffin and Donald W. Sherburne. New York: Free Press [Corrected Edition].

Wiesel, Elie. 1982. *The Accident.* Translated by Anne Borchardt. New York: Bantam Books.

Wiesel, Elie. 2006. *Night.* Translated by Marion Wiesel. New York: Hill and Wang.

Winnicott, D. W. 1958. *Collected Papers: Through Paediatrics to Psycho-Analysis.* New York: Basic Books.

Winnicott, D. W. 1965a. *The Family and Individual Development.* London: Tavistock.

Winnicott, D. W. 1965b. *The Maturational Processes and the Facilitating Environment.* New York: International Universities Press.

Winnicott, D. W. 1971. *Playing and Reality.* London and New York: Routledge.

Winnicott, D. W. 1986. *Home Is Where We Start From.* New York: W. W. Norton.

Winnicott, D. W. 1987. "Communication between Infant and Mother, and Mother and Infant, Compared and Contrasted." In *Babies and Their Mothers*, pp. 89–103. Edited by Claire Winnicott, Ray Shepherd, and Madeleine Davis. London: Free Association Books.

Winnicott, D. W. 1989. *Psycho-Analytic Explorations.* Edited by Claire Winnicott, Ray Shepherd, and Madeleine Davis. Cambridge, MA: Harvard University Press.

Zimbardo, Phillip, et al. 1983. "Interpersonal Dynamics in a Simulated Prison." *International Journal of Criminology and Penology*, 1: 69–97.

Index